sheds
AND GARAGES

By Rick Peters and the Editors of Sunset Books, Menlo Park, California

SUNSET BOOKS

VICE PRESIDENT AND GENERAL MANAGER: Richard A. Smeby
VICE PRESIDENT AND EDITORIAL DIRECTOR: Bob Doyle
PRODUCTION DIRECTOR: Lory Day
OPERATIONS DIRECTOR: Rosann Sutherland
RETAIL SALES DEVELOPMENT MANAGER: Linda Barker
EXECUTIVE EDITOR: Bridget Biscotti Bradley
ART DIRECTOR: Vasken Guiragossian

STAFF FOR THIS BOOK:

MANAGING EDITOR: Dave Toht
SENIOR EDITOR, SUNSET BOOKS: Mara Wildfeuer
WRITER: Rick Peters
DESIGN: Jean DeVaty
ASSOCIATE DESIGNER: Rebecca Anderson
DESIGN ASSISTANT: Sarah Tibbot
PHOTO EDITOR: Jane Martin
PRINCIPAL PHOTOGRAPHER: Christophter Vendetta
ILLUSTRATOR: Troy Doolittle
COPY EDITOR: Barbara McIntosh Webb
PROOFREADER: David Sweet
INDEXER: Nanette Cardon

Cover: Photography by Christopher Vendetta (top, bottom middle, bottom right); Dan Stultz (bottom left).

Additional photography credits: Alan and Linda Detrick 1, 4, 7 right, 9 top right; Frank Gaglione 42; John Granen 74, 82; Dency Kane 3 top, 6 top, 7 top, 9 top, 11 bottom right, 12 top, 12 bottom; Robert Perron 6 left, 8 top, 10 top, 11 top, 11 bottom; Karen Bussolini 6 bottom, landscape design by Peter Woerner; 9 bottom right, landscape design by John Scofield; Judy White 2, 8 left, 9 bottom, 12 center; Terry Wild Studio, Inc. 10 bottom, 8 bottom, 11 top right, 22; Jerry Pavia 12 left; Dan Stultz 70, 78.

10 9 8 7 6 5 4 3
First printing January, 2004
Copyright ©2004
Sunset Publishing Corporation,
Menlo Park, CA 94025.

ISBN: 0-376-01376-1
Library of Congress Control Number: 2003110992
Printed in the United States.

For additional copies of *Sheds & Garages* or any other Sunset book, call 1-800-526-5111 or visit us at www.sunset.com.

CONTENTS

a gallery of sheds, garages, and barns

WHILE IT MAY BE THE MOST FUNCTIONAL BUILDING on your property, a shed or a barn (even a garage, the modern equivalent of a barn) can have a distinctly romantic quality. Perhaps that's because it harkens to times of hands-on simplicity, when gardening and the care of animals were part of our daily rhythm. These utilitarian structures carry associations of a no-frills, form meets function, rural lifestyle when pure usefulness had its own beauty. ■ Such beauty can complement a home and its surrounding landscape, turning a humble structure into an attractive focal point. A shed, garage, or barn can be a destination for paths and a centerpiece for plantings, trellises—even a decorative pond. ■ Perhaps best of all, an outbuilding is ideal for a budding carpenter. Its basic function is forgiving of less-than-perfect joinery and often requires no plumbing, wiring, or interior wall surfacing. And it can provide the chance to experiment with unusual combinations of colors and materials.

sheds

Whether it's a place for potting plants, storing gardening tools, keeping firewood out of the wet, or forging the great American novel, a shed is a fundamentally simple structure. Depending on local codes, its foundation can be as simple as a pair of skids (page 98) or as permanent as a concrete slab (pages 25–26). Even a landing by an ornamental pool (right) can host a shed.

▲ **ELEGANT ORNAMENTATION** *has its place in shed design. Even though sheds are simple in function, they can be little gems of detailing, echoing in miniature the architectural pedigree of your home.*

▶ *A **SALTBOX-STYLE ROOF** shelters firewood and is a pleasing companion for a larger shed suitable for a woodworking shop or artist's studio. An unpainted exterior melds well with the rustic setting.*

◀ *FRENCH DOORS CAN BRIGHTEN* a shed—especially if artificial light is unavailable. Sheds provide an ideal opportunity for using secondhand and salvage doors whose size and style may not measure up for installation in a home.

▲ *A GAMBREL-ROOFED GARDEN SHED* with a double door that allows easy access for anything from a tiller to a riding mower, this barnlike shed keeps tool storage close to the garden. While more complex to build than a shed or gable roof, a gambrel roof bulges at the sides to provide more headroom—just as it was originally conceived to make room for more hay.

▶ **A RAMP AND DOUBLE DOORS** make it easy to wheel garden and lawn-care equipment into the shed. The roof overhang shelters the interior when the doors are open and provides the opportunity for some stylish brackets.

▲ **BOARD-AND-BATTEN SIDING** was originally a low-cost alternative to clapboard siding for keeping the weather out—the battens covered the gaps between the boards. Today it has appeal as a handsome, traditional cladding.

▶ **UNCONVENTIONAL MATERIALS,** like log ends set in mortar, fill the half-timbered structure of this shed. The result is a rustic, storybook look that beautifully complements a free-ranging garden.

SKYLIGHTS ARE IDEAL SOURCES OF LIGHT *for sheds without electricity. And if you are clever with trim, a shed can sport various-sized salvaged windows.*

A CUPOLA AND A TRELLIS, *combined with a multipaned window, make this shed as beautiful as it is useful.*

TREE LIMBS STAND IN AS ORNATE POSTS *in this freewheeling retreat. Part of the fun of shed building is improvising with whatever materials you find at hand.*

This shed adapts to the site as well, nestling in close to a stream and its steppingstone path.

DECEPTIVELY SIMPLE, *this shed combines sliding double doors, ideal for hauling out lawn and garden equipment, with a single door that provides easy access for fetching hand tools. And why plunk down money for store-bought door handles when pieces of driftwood work just as well?*

garages

A well-designed garage not only shelters cars and provides storage, it complements the architecture of the house. Even a basic garage can mimic house details—like eaves depth, siding and trim style, and window design—and meld them into its setting.

▶ **CLERESTORY WINDOWS** illuminate second-story space on this garage and provide stunning architectural detail to an otherwise basic garage. High-pitched gable roofs offer plenty of upstairs space—a gambrel roof provides even more.

▲ **NO MERE BREEZEWAY,** this link between house and garage is set apart with a portico porch to become a main entrance. Graceful arches fronting the garage provide sheltered access.

▶ **A GOOD NEIGHBOR,** this garage melds beautifully with a nearby barn by borrowing a cupola and barnlike siding and trim. Door openings echo the gambrel roof of the barn.

▼ **A RAMPED ENTRYWAY** to this multifunction garage takes advantage of a hilly site to add a lower level. A hip roof can be a challenge to frame, but it provides a distinctive silhouette.

▲ **EVEN A GARAGE CAN HAVE A ROMANTIC SIDE** when plantings and a rustic rake are used to link it to an adjacent garden. Weathered siding helps mellow it into its site.

◀ **A PROFILE THAT COMPLEMENTS** the basic shape of the house is another way to be sure your garage will be an attractive addition. A deep gable roof and subtly arched doors are all this garage needs to be an asset to its setting.

barns

Once shelter for animals and crops, barns are now multi-function structures that house workshops, studios, vehicles, and gardening tools.

◀ **CLASSIC BARN CONSTRUCTION** includes board-and-batten siding, shake shingles, and doors fabricated on-site.

▼ **FIREWOOD FINDS A HOME** in a lean-to add-on to a barn. The lightly arched bays are relatively simple to construct and add an appealing feature.

▲ **WHETHER IN PASTURE OR GARDEN,** a barn is a stately, and utilitarian, presence. Barns offer space galore—room for tools and machines, a potting area, and gobs of miscellaneous storage.

▶ **A DESTINATION,** this barn begs to be explored. It demonstrates that a barn can add a focal point that is both beautiful and useful. It's well worth the effort to choose a site that not only is close to the chores but, like this bend in a stream, calls out for an architectural feature.

design and construction

A SHED IS A HUMBLE STRUCTURE, so it's tempting to buy a pile of lumber and slap the thing together in a weekend. However, for a structure that will look good and function well, plan ahead. Think through the siting, as much to meet your own needs as to satisfy local codes and zoning laws. ■ Anticipate the use to which the shed will be put—now and in the future. As always, we tend to need more space as time goes on, so try to imagine what the future holds—it's hardly more labor-intensive and only moderately more expensive to make the structure somewhat larger from the get-go. ■ For style, key off your home and any nearby out-buildings. Or, go in the opposite direction, building a structure in a contrasting style, creating an opportunity for using unusual materials. ■ The projects found on pages 34–94 offer detailed points of departure for building your shed, garage, or barn. Each equips you with the essentials for planning and constructing a structure that meets your specific needs.

the big picture

Somewhere between our inside living space and the great outdoors is an in-between zone—not home, but not outside. This zone is where we put our cars, our garden tools, and our animals. Sometimes, this zone is where we find some private space for potting plants or repairing a boat. Whether we want to store a riding mower, build a patio bench, or stable a Shetland pony, we turn to sheds, garages, and barns to provide protected space.

ASSESSING NEEDS

What do you need space for? Have you always wanted a place to make pottery? Or do you just need somewhere to stash the snowblower? You may find that a combination of work and storage space would be best for you.

You won't know for sure until you take the first step: assessing your needs. What, exactly, do you want your structure to do, both now and in the future? List every possible use you can think of. Will the structure be used just for storage? Or will you want a workspace? And if so, what type of work will you be doing?

Once you've defined the function of the structure, the next step is to determine its size. If it's strictly storage you're after, make a list of everything that you'll be putting inside it, now and in the future. What about the lawn furniture? And the outdoor grill?

Bikes? Toys? Figuring future needs is always a challenge, but well worth the effort. Will you be buying a larger lawn mower in the future? Will the kids' bicycles step up in size over time? Is there another vehicle in your future? Maybe a boat? It's a lot easier to build larger now for future needs than it is to expand an existing structure later. The tough part is being realistic. See page 15 for general spacing guidelines.

PLANNING WORK SPACE

If you'll be doing work inside the structure, think about how much space you'll need to move about comfortably. Will you be working alone? Or with others? Next, what utilities, if any, do you need? Hot and cold running water? Electricity? Heat? And don't forget about lighting. Although windows will provide delightful natural light during the day, they won't be much use in the evening.

CHOOSING A STYLE

After you've decided the structure's function and size, you can turn your attention to appearance. There are two basic roads to travel here. One is to make the structure blend in and match existing structures as much as possible. This can be done by using similar materials for siding, roofing, windows, and doors. Matching the roof lines helps as well. For example, a shed with

This shed was planned not only to provide vital storage space, but also to be a delightful backyard feature. The louvered cupola looks great and provides ventilation.

a hip roof will look better with a hip-roofed house than a gambrel-style shed will (see pages 17 and 20–21 for more on roofing styles).

Your other appearance option is to ignore the style and design of existing structures. Since the new structure is likely to be free-standing (versus attached), you can have some fun with it. Have you always yearned for a Victorian house? Then how about a Victorian shed? Some home-owners like to think of their outbuildings as conversation pieces; it's all a matter of personal preference. To get some ideas for the look of your structure, drive around town and note any that strike your fancy. Likewise, page through home magazines for ideas. Try to identify what it is about each that you like. Is it the style? The roof line? Siding? Maybe it's the landscaping. The better you define what you like, the easier it'll be to decide on a final look.

typical spacing

A tape measure and a pad of graph paper are indispensable for identifying spacing needs inside any structure. Start by drawing an outline of the intended structure on graph paper as close to scale as possible, using a scale of ¼ inch equaling 1 foot works well. Then begin measuring everything that you intend to store inside: cars, bikes, boxes, workbenches, lawn mowers, etc. Next, think about how all of this will be stored. Try to envision wall racks and bins for garden tools and sports equipment, and shelving for potting supplies and small items. Then pencil these inside your structure's outlines and check the recommended spacing at right to make sure you've got plenty of room to move around.

SHED SPACING ▶

Allow at least a 12-inch-zone around lawn mowers, bikes, and boxes so that you can walk around them with ease. Also, think about how you'll remove one piece of equipment without disturbing the others. This is particularly important if you're storing a riding lawn mower or other big item, as these often block access to the rest of the things stored inside. One way around this is to offset the door to one side of the shed and then store the lawn mower against the side wall nearest the door.

GARAGE SPACING ▼

With today's wider vehicles, it's crucial that you measure them and maintain adequate spacing so you can get in and out comfortably, as well as walk around inside the garage. Because most garages are also used for storage, make sure there's adequate space for this. Also, consider traffic patterns inside to make sure that there's convenient access to car doors.

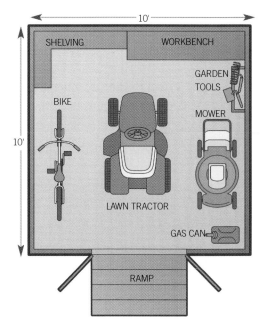

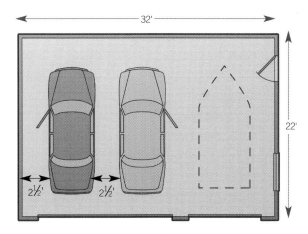

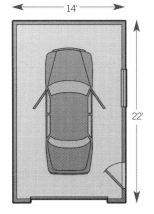

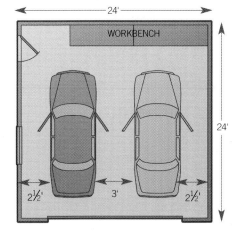

DRIVEWAY OPTIONS ▼

A new garage usually means adding a new driveway. In addition to the standard straight-to-the-doors design, you can opt for a turnaround area (below left) or additional parking space (below right). In most cases, short driveways are sized to match the width of the garage. Longer driveways, on the other hand, are usually only single-car-width to hold down the paving costs.

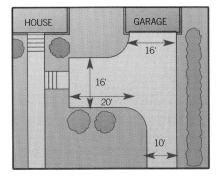

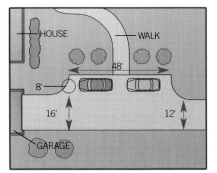

location and code

Where you locate a new structure will have a huge impact on how well it functions, as well as affecting the overall look of your property. In many areas, zoning restrictions and local building codes regulate where you can place your structure, as well as define its maximum dimensions. The extent of the restrictions depends on your town and on the type and size of your structure. To find out, consult with your building inspector. He or she will advise whether you'll need a building permit and inspection to make sure the structure meets minimum code requirements.

In some areas, structures below a certain square footage—typically 100–120 square feet—are considered accessory buildings and don't require a permit. Also, structures built on temporary foundations such as skids (page 90),

which can be moved, might not require a permit either. Permits may seem a nuisance, but they're in your best interest. An inspection can ensure that the structure you build will be sturdy and safe—now and in the future.

BEING A GOOD NEIGHBOR

In terms of outbuildings, zoning restrictions are designed to prevent homeowners from encroaching on their neighbors. They're sometimes also enforced to create a unified look in an area, especially in historic sections and in neighborhoods with homeowners associations. The most commonly enforced restrictions are lot coverage, setbacks, easements, and building height (see below). Lot coverage limits how much of the property can be covered by buildings. A setback

defines how close a structure can be built to another structure and to the property lines. An easement is an area that must be left accessible to people other than the homeowner (such as space near a power pole for utility-worker access). Building height may be restricted as well. Apply for a variance if you feel your plans are within the spirit, if not the letter, of the law.

CONSIDER TRAFFIC

Once you've identified any restrictions, you can pick the final spot for your new structure. Think about access and traffic flow in all four seasons. What might seem an ideal spot in the summer might be inaccessible in the winter. Likewise, trees that provide privacy in the summer may leave your structure exposed in the fall. For workspaces, consider the views you'll have out of the windows of the structure. Finally, walk around and observe how the structure will be viewed from your house or property line.

DRIVEWAY

BARN

SIZE LIMITATION

HEIGHT RESTRICTION

HOUSE

DRIVEWAY

SIDE YARD MINIMUM

SHED

GARAGE

SETBACK MINIMUM

HEIGHT RESTRICTION

IDENTIFYING RESTRICTIONS
To assure your new structure will be neighborly, municipalities have setback and height restrictions. To determine compliance, sketch the site, with measurements, and check with your building department.

shed styles

There are five major shed styles to choose from: gable, gambrel, lean-to, saltbox, and hip. There are variations of each type, but these are the basic shapes. Although each style generally has a rectangular footprint, what sets the styles apart is the roof line, which is how the roof is framed and pitched.

GABLE On a gable shed, the two halves of the roof join together in the classic triangular shape. Gable roofs are simple and economical

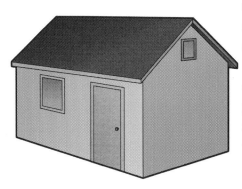

to build and offer superior load-bearing and drainage capabilities. A hip roof (see page 21) is formed by sloping the ends of a gable roof toward the center. This creates an overhang around all four sides of the structure.

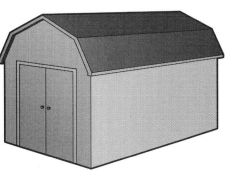

GAMBREL A gambrel roof (so named after the hindquarter of a horse) is basically a gable roof with two slopes or pitches on each side. Although more complex to frame, it offers significantly more headroom and storage space than a gable roof.

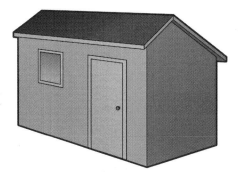

SALTBOX A saltbox, or offset-ridge shed, is similar to a gable except that storage space is added to the front and capped with a narrow roof section. This creates a ridge line that's offset from the center—and also surprisingly more space inside.

LEAN-TO A lean-to roof design (also referred to as a shed roof) is inexpensive and easy to frame. But because of the slope, headroom inside varies greatly from front to back.

BASIC ANATOMY

The construction of most sheds is the same; the difference primarily is how the roof is framed. Sheds are built like a house—just smaller. Like a house, a shed rests on a foundation to give it a solid base. This can be temporary skids (as shown here), or more permanent poured footings. Rim joists run around the perimeter of the foundation and are spanned by floor joists covered with structural plywood. The walls are built from 2-by lumber in sections, and secured to the floor and tied together above with top plates. Rafters run between the top plates and the ridge board and are sheathed with plywood. This is then covered with roofing felt and shingles. Windows and doors are installed in the rough openings, and the exterior walls are covered with exterior-grade sheathing, siding, or shingles. Finally, trim is added for a finished look.

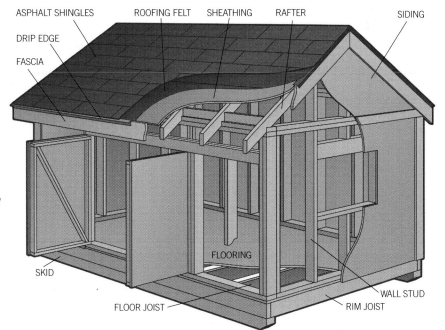

shed makeovers

Do you want to match a shed to your existing structures? Are you after a totally different look? Do you plan to make over an existing shed? You can create almost any look to meet any of these objectives by selecting the right materials, fixtures, and trim for the exterior. To illustrate this, we've made over the same gable shed in four distinctly different styles: Arts and Crafts, Victorian, Colonial Revival, and Tudor. Virtually any other style can be mimicked by identifying the architectural features that the style is famous for, and applying them to your structure.

▲ **ARTS AND CRAFTS** The Arts and Crafts—or Mission—style, is based on a movement popularized by Gustav Stickley in the United States that began in the 1890s and lasted for around 20 years. The style embraces simplicity and honesty in construction. Bungalow homes in this style are characterized by large overhangs, lower-pitched roofs, exposed eaves, roof brackets, and multiple siding materials. Copper light fixtures often adorn the exterior, typically with mica or stained glass to diffuse the light.

◀ **VICTORIAN** Known for its ornamentation and complexity, the Victorian style (often called Queen Anne) was developed in Great Britain and became an instant success in America. Irregularly shaped windows, stained glass, complex roofs, and filigree create an interesting exterior. Fanciful scrollwork, delicate spindles, and turned columns, along with varying siding materials, offer plenty of opportunity to spice up the exterior with contrasting colors that make the details "pop."

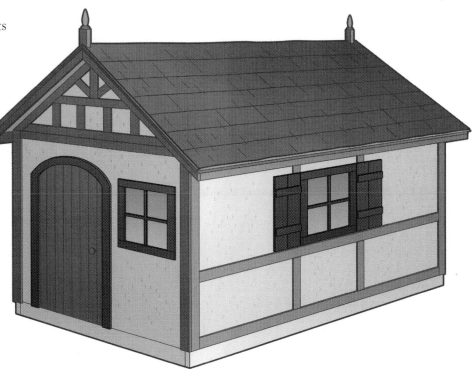

◀ **COLONIAL REVIVAL**
The Colonial Revival style became popular in the late 19th century, drawing its inspiration from Georgian Colonial architecture. This style can be identified by its symmetrical facades, where windows are arranged flanking a central doorway. Half columns typically surround the door as well, and most entryway doors are topped with a fanlight, like the one shown here. Sidelights for the entryway door are also common. Windows are typically a combination of six, eight, nine, or 12 panes of glass in each sash.

▶ **TUDOR** The Tudor style has its roots in 16th-century England, some buildings even mimicking medieval cottages, complete with thatched roofs. A Tudor building features lavish use of stone, heavy chimneys, and decorative half-timbering. Tudor structures typically feature steeply pitched roofs with prominent cross gables. The faux half-timbering used these days is strictly decorative, and merely suggests the underlying structural framework. In many cases, the exterior between the half-timbering and cross gables is covered with stucco, patterned brick, or stone veneer.

garage styles

Because a garage is usually attached to or very near a house, it's best if the garage style mimics that of the house. The four most common styles are: gable, reverse gable, hip, and gambrel. Just as with sheds, most garages have rectangular or square footprints, and the main difference in style has to do with how the roof is framed.

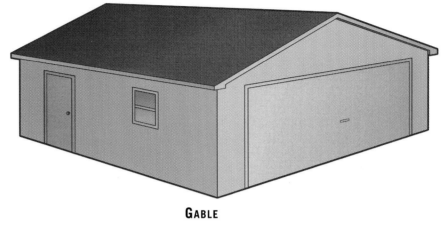

GABLE

GABLE Gable-style garages (above right), where the two halves of the roof are symmetrical and join together to form a triangle, are the most common type of garage built. The garage door is installed in one of the gabled ends. These structures are easy to frame and economical to build. They also provide excellent load-bearing capabilities as well as good drainage.

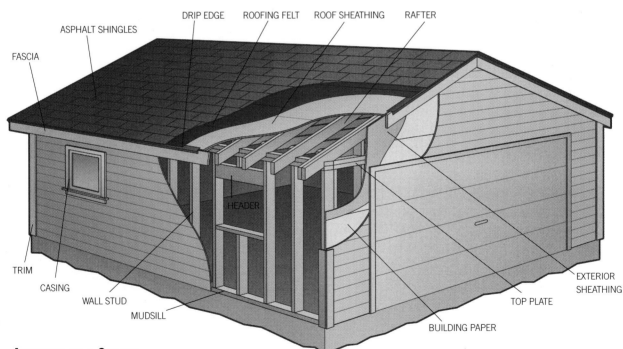

ASPHALT SHINGLES · DRIP EDGE · ROOFING FELT · ROOF SHEATHING · RAFTER · FASCIA · HEADER · TRIM · CASING · WALL STUD · MUDSILL · BUILDING PAPER · TOP PLATE · EXTERIOR SHEATHING

ANATOMY OF A GARAGE

Because garages are typically much larger than sheds, building permits are usually required and the structure must be built to code. In many ways, garage construction is very similar to that of a house. The foundation for the garage is usually some form of slab (see pages 98–100 for more on foundation options). Walls are typically built in sections and raised one at a time. They are braced temporarily upright and secured to the foundation with a mudsill that's attached with concrete anchors.

Rough openings are placed wherever doors or windows are to be installed; headers at the top replace the support that would have been provided by the wall studs. Ceiling joists span the walls and hold them together; rafters are attached to ceiling joists and the ridge board to form the roof. The rafters are covered with sheathing, roofing felt, and shingles. Windows and doors are installed, and exterior sheathing, siding, or shingles are added, along with the exterior trim to complete the garage.

REVERSE-GABLE A reverse-gable garage is identical to a gable garage with one very important difference. Instead of locating the door in one of the gabled ends, the door is installed under the eaves on one of the long walls. A reverse-gable garage has the same features of the gable version; the main reason this design is chosen over a gable often concerns how the garage lies in relation to the street. For example, if the gable of the planned garage aligns with the gable on the home, you can run the driveway straight in from the street if you use the reverse gable design. In that case, if you were to choose a standard gable, you'd need to run a driveway around to the gabled end—requiring a larger lot.

HIP This roof style is identified by gabled ends that lean in toward the center. These ends may run all the way to the center, creating a pyramid-like roof, or they may run partially in, leaving a flat portion near the center. In either case, the overhang runs around the entire perimeter and offers the best protection against the elements for you and your garage. The reason they're not more common is that the complex roof line is much more difficult to frame, involving scores of compound miter cuts. Also on the downside—this roof type offers less upstairs storage space than a gable or gambrel roof.

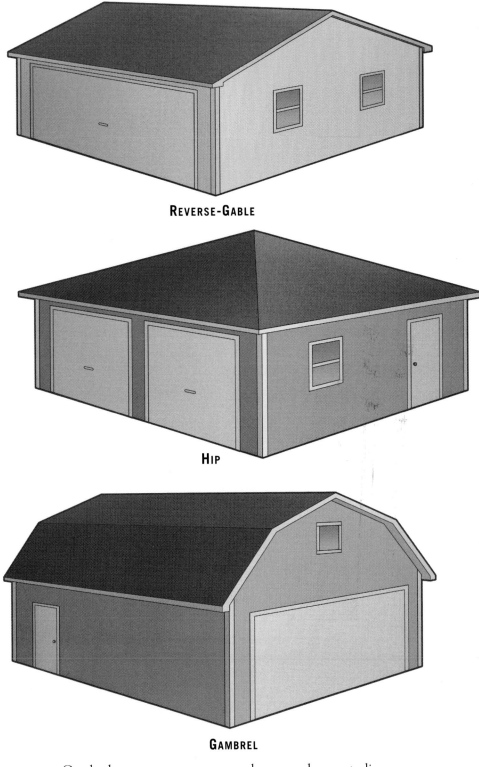

REVERSE-GABLE

HIP

GAMBREL

GAMBREL Gambrel garages are basically gable garages with two pitches on each slope. This creates additional headroom and space that can be pressed into service as storage, or to provide a work area such as a studio or workshop. The roof framing is more complex than for a gable roof (though simpler than for a hip roof), but the additional space often makes it worth the effort.

barn construction

Because barns are often much larger than garages and houses, several different techniques are used for their construction. The most common are pole construction, stick-framed, and timber framing. Which construction technique is used depends primarily on how the barn will be used. For example, the dirt floor of a pole barn may be perfect for housing animals, but isn't a good choice for a workshop or studio, where a dry floor is required. Here you'd be better served by a slab foundation and either a stick- or timber-framed structure.

Framed much like a gable garage (page 20) though with a taller first floor, a stick-built gable barn is simpler to construct than a gambrel barn. Stained and sealed clapboard siding is an option that is low-maintenance and gentle on the eye.

STICK-FRAMED GAMBREL BARN

A stick-framed barn uses conventional 2-by construction methods. The main difference is that the framing members are usually stouter and longer to span greater distances. Although simple to build, the higher roof and wider wall spans often require the use of a crane to lift and set sections in place. Stick-framed barns are usually built on a slab foundation. And just as with a garage or shed, wall sections are built and then raised into position. Then they're secured to the foundation with a mudsill and tied together above with top plates. Barn roofs are often built using premade trusses (see page 111 for more on these). The gambrel-style roof is by far the most popular choice for barns, as it offers maximum storage space above.

POLE BARN A pole barn is the least expensive and quickest way to build a barn. Poles are driven into the ground, and horizontal members called girts join the poles together. Vertical siding is then applied to enclose the space. Roof framing is simple, as rafters are secured to the girts on top of the poles and to the ridge girt.

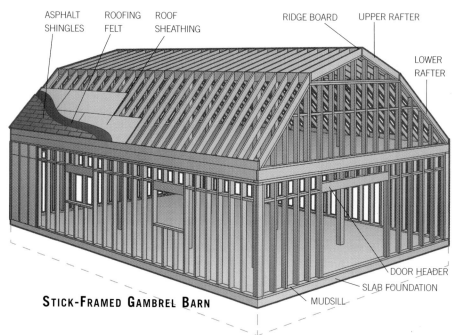

ASPHALT SHINGLES   ROOFING FELT   ROOF SHEATHING   RIDGE BOARD   UPPER RAFTER   LOWER RAFTER   DOOR HEADER   SLAB FOUNDATION   MUDSILL

STICK-FRAMED GAMBREL BARN

The poles set into the ground can be round, unmilled trees or square posts. The beauty of this method is that no foundation is required. That's not to say that you can't add one. This is best done by adding a framed floor above the ground to remove concerns about flooding and vermin. This flexibility in foundations and flooring makes a pole barn the ideal choice for sloped sites—no excavation is required.

TIMBER-FRAMED BARN If you want a barn that will last a lifetime and then some, choose the timber framing method of construction. With this method, large, heavy timbers are joined together using age-old joinery techniques such as the mortise-and-tenon. Besides creating incredibly sturdy structures, timber framing lets you span great distances without any center supports. Because the timbers used are so stout, wall studs are not necessary for sup-

port. This allows the use of insulated wall panels (often called stress skin panels), made by sandwiching insulation between interior and exterior sheathing. This creates sections of uninterrupted insulation. The disadvantage: timber framing is a highly skilled craft and should not be attempted by anyone without training (there

are a number of timber-framing schools nationwide). Also, the timbers themselves are heavy; when assembled into wall sections, they require either a complicated set of ropes and pulleys and a lot of help to lift them into position, or else a crane.

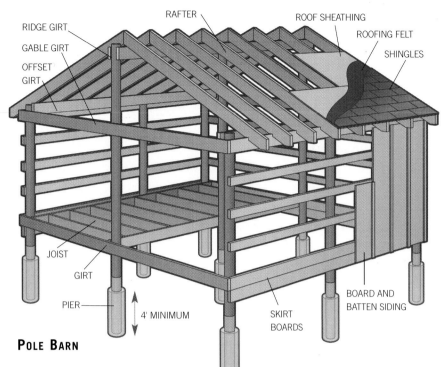

RIDGE GIRT
GABLE GIRT
OFFSET GIRT
RAFTER
ROOF SHEATHING
ROOFING FELT
SHINGLES
JOIST
GIRT
PIER
4' MINIMUM
SKIRT BOARDS
BOARD AND BATTEN SIDING

POLE BARN

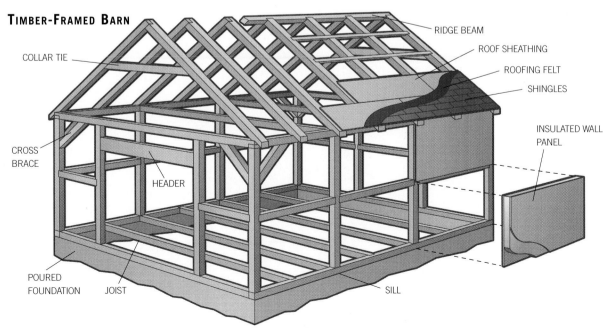

TIMBER-FRAMED BARN

COLLAR TIE
CROSS BRACE
HEADER
POURED FOUNDATION
JOIST
SILL
RIDGE BEAM
ROOF SHEATHING
ROOFING FELT
SHINGLES
INSULATED WALL PANEL

building a shed

Whether you're building a stick-framed shed, garage, or barn, the construction methods are much the same. What will be different is the materials you use for the larger buildings; you'll be using stouter, longer lumber—and more of it. Framing members need to be beefier to span longer distances and to accept thicker insulation. A wide structure may require 2×10s instead of 2×8s to span the walls without sagging. A garage built in the Midwest that also serves as a workshop will use 2×6s for the wall framing instead of 2×4s to hold the thicker fiberglass insulation needed in cold winters.

The type of foundation you install will also depend on the size of the structure. Most sheds can be built on skids, precast piers, or poured footings (pages 98–100). These foundations can be tackled by the average homeowner, but the slab foundation shown here is best installed by professionals, as it requires deep footings, reinforced rod to prevent cracks, and a load or two from a cement mixer.

The first step in building any structure is to have the building plans and site plan approved by your local building inspector (see page 16). Ask what they need to inspect and when. When everything is approved, you can prepare the site and start gathering your materials.

BUILDING A KIT SHED

If you like the idea of a new shed but would rather not build one from scratch, consider a "kit" shed. There are two basic types of shed kits available: parts kits and prefabricated kits. With a parts kit, you get a set of plans and most (if not all) of the materials. You need only cut the pieces to size and assemble the shed. See page 128 for a list of kit manufacturers.

With a prefabricated kit, sections come already assembled and attach together to form the floor, walls, and roof. For an additional fee, most kit manufacturers offer an assembly service, dispatching a crew to put the shed together for you.

This handsome gable shed is straightforward to build. See pages 18–19 for ways to improvise on this basic design.

24

1 Lay Out the Foundation

If there's one part of building a shed, garage, or barn that's worth some extra time, it's laying out and creating the foundation. Small errors can telegraph into the finished structure, causing even larger problems later. Begin laying out your foundation, using batter boards and stakes (batter boards are pointed 2 × 4s driven into the ground and spanned with 1 × 4s). Consult your shed plan, and roughly locate the footings with a stake. Then position pairs of batter boards at right angles to each other about 18 inches behind each stake. Stretch a mason's line between adjacent corners, and wrap the line around nails driven into the batter boards. Adjust the nails on the batter boards to align the mason's line with the stakes locating the footings. Use a 3-4-5 triangle (page 103) to make sure the lines are perpendicular.

2 Dig Footings

Temporarily loosen the mason's lines so they don't interfere as you dig the footing. In most areas, you will need to dig at least 12 inches below the frost line—check with your building inspector for footing dimensions. If you're installing a slab (shown), excavate at least 4 inches of soil beneath the slab and add 4 inches of pea gravel for drainage. Then dig a 12- to 16-inch-deep trench around the perimeter for a 12-inch-wide footing at the bottom (see page 99).

3 Build Forms

Slab foundations use forms to define the sides of the slab. These are 2-by boards held in place with stakes. If you're having a slab installed by a contractor, they'll build the forms for you. If you're installing poured footings, see pages 98–100. Before you pour concrete for a slab foundation, add rebar and wire mesh to help prevent cracking. Set #5 rebar on bricks placed in the bottom of the trench. This raises the rebar so the concrete can flow around it. Lay a 6-mil vapor barrier over the slab section and then place #10 reinforcing mesh over the slab, keeping it 2 inches from the forms. Insert bricks under the mesh to raise it as you did for the rebar.

4 Pour Concrete

Now you're ready to pour. If you're pouring your own footings, see page 100. On a slab foundation, the concrete truck will arrive with a load of concrete and, with the help of the contractor crew, these folks will quickly pour it into the form.

5 Screed It Level

Once the concrete has been poured, it's leveled or "striked" with the aid of a screed—typically a long, straight 2×4 or 2×6. The screed spans the form from side to side. As it's dragged across the top, it levels the concrete. After striking, smooth the concrete with a bull float by dragging it carefully over the concrete (inset). Once the finishing is complete, mist the slab with water and cover it with a layer of plastic. Keep the surface moist for two to three days.

6 Install Anchors

With a poured footing or slab foundation, the shed attaches to the footings or slab via anchors set into the concrete. For maximum holding power, these are typically shaped like a J. To install the anchors on poured footings, reposition the mason's lines on the batter boards and use a plumb bob to mark the anchor location in the footing. Push an anchor into the wet concrete and wiggle it to get the concrete to fill in around it. Adjust its position so it's directly centered under the plumb bob and is plumb. On a slab, snap a chalk line the desired distance in from the edge and then measure and mark anchor locations per your plans.

7 Lay Out Top and Bottom Plates

Once the foundation is complete, you can start framing the walls, one of the most satisfying parts of building a shed. The best way to make sure that wall studs align is to lay out the top and bottom plates at the same time; these form the top and bottom of the walls. (Note: On slab foundations, the bottom plate is called a mudsill and is usually pressure-treated wood.) Start by measuring and cutting plates for one wall at a time—make sure to choose lumber as

straight as possible for these critical parts. Align the plate ends and screw them together temporarily. Set the plates on edge and, measuring from one end, make a mark at 1½ inches and then at 15¼ inches (for 16-inch-on-center spacing) or 23¼ inches (for 24-inch-on-center spacing). Use a combination square and a pencil to continue these marks across both plates. Then measure and mark a line every 16 or 24 inches from these lines, continuing the full length of the plates. Make an **X** on the appropriate side of each line to indicate stud placement.

8 Build Walls

Remove the screws and separate the top and bottom plate. (On a slab foundation, first position the mudsill on the slab and transfer the anchors' locations onto the mudsill; drill appropriate-sized holes for the anchors to pass through.) Then cut sufficient studs to length for the wall, and end-nail them to the top and bottom plates, taking care to position the studs over the **X**'s you made on the plates. Cut a scrap of 1 × 4 to reach from corner to corner of the completed wall, to serve as a brace and to keep the wall square. Attach it to one corner and measure diagonals. Adjust the wall until the diagonal measurements are equal, and then secure the other end of the 1 × 4 brace.

FRAMED FLOORS

If your plans call for a framed floor, add post bases to the footings and either beams or rim joists. Post bases are metal fittings that accept dimension lumber. They bolt to the anchors you set in the footings. Place a post base over each anchor, and use a framing square to check that the post base is aligned with the mason's lines. Tighten the nuts fully. Add beams or rim joists and secure them with lag screws.

Span the beams or rim joists with floor joists placed every 16 or 24 inches. When all are installed, measure diagonally across both sets of opposing corners to check for square—the measurements should be the same. If they're not, loosen the nuts securing the post bases and push on the longer dimension corner to bring the floor square. Measure again. If it's square, retighten the post base nuts.

To add flooring, apply a bead of construction adhesive to the joists. Position a full sheet of ¾-inch tongue-and-groove plywood on the joists so it's flush with the edges. Secure with nails or screws every 6 inches. Start the next row with a half sheet to offset the seams, and finish adding plywood.

braces to the rim joists adjacent to the wall you're raising. Then, with the aid of a helper or two, lift the wall section up and set it into place so the bottom plate is flush along the entire front edge of the flooring and so the end of the wall aligns with the end of the floor. (On a slab foundation, make sure all the anchors pass through the mudsill.)

11 Level and Brace Wall

Use a level to adjust the wall section as needed to bring it into plumb. When everything looks good, have a helper secure the other end of the scrap wood braces to the wall section with nails or screws. After you've done this, take the time to double-check for plumb before moving on to the next wall. Quite often the act of securing the wall to the brace will shift it out of plumb; readjust as necessary.

9 Frame Rough Openings

If the wall section that you're building includes windows or doors, you'll need to frame rough openings. Cut king, jack, and cripple studs (see page 101) per your plan along with a header for each opening (see also page 107). Attach the king studs between the top and bottom plate and secure the jack studs to these. Place the header on top of the jack studs and toenail it to the jack and king studs. Complete the rough opening by installing a sill and cripple studs as needed.

10 Raise the Wall Section

Before you raise a wall, temporarily attach a pair of scrap wood

12 Secure Wall Section to Floor

Attach the wall section to the floor by driving nails or screws every 16 inches or so through the bottom plate and into the floor. About half of the fasteners should penetrate into the rim joists, and the other half go into the floor joists. (For a slab foundation, add washers and thread on nuts—don't tighten until all the walls are in place and leveled.) Frame the next wall and continue until all walls are raised. Don't drive nails through the bottom plate in a doorway—this piece will be cut away when framing is done.

13 Secure Corners

When all the walls are in place, you'll need to add extra studs at the corners so you can securely attach the wall sections to each other. Space these studs away from the end stud with filler blocks. Then start at one corner and nail together the end studs with 16-penny nails. Repeat at the next corner. It's a good idea here to check for level and plumb one more time, as the walls may have shifted slightly. Remove the temporary scrap wood braces.

14 Install Double Top Plate

The tops of the walls are fixed together by adding another top plate. This double top plate creates a rigid structure that will help support the roof. Cut the double top plates to length so that they overlap the top plate joints. Secure the double top plate to the top plate with 10-penny nails every 16 inches or so. Also, drive in two nails at the ends of the plates that overlap intersecting walls. Use a hand saw or reciprocating saw to remove the bottom plate in any door openings.

Depending on your shed plan, you may or may not need to add ceiling joists to span the walls. If you do, cut them to length and install them now. Small shed plans may not call for ceiling joists at all, or they may use collar ties. Most roof framing is based on the gable roof, where rafters are spaced at 16- or 24-inch increments and secured to the double top plate at their bottom and to the ridge board at the top. (See pages 110–112 for more on roof framing.)

15 Make a Rafter Template

The most precise and efficient way to cut rafters is to make a rafter template from a piece of rafter stock (typically 2 × 4s or 2 × 6s for sheds). Consult your plans and carefully lay out the top and bottom plumb cuts along with the bird's mouth—a notch that's cut so the angled rafter can rest on the double top plate (see page 114). After you've made the template, cut two rafters and test the fit by holding them temporarily in position with a scrap of 2-by material in between to serve as a ridge board. If everything looks good, cut the remaining rafters.

16 Lay Out Rafters

Starting at one end of the building, measure and mark the position of the rafters on the double top plates, making sure to start at the same end on both sides that you used to lay out the wall studs; this ensures that the rafters will be installed directly over the studs. Mark an X on the appropriate side of each line. Trim the ridge board to length and transfer the rafter layout from the double top plates to the ridge board.

17 Install Rafters

End-nail the first rafter to the ridge board and toenail the second rafter to this. Lift this assembly into place so the bird's-mouth notches fit over the double top plates. Have a helper support the opposite end of the ridge board, check to make sure the ridge board is level, and add a brace to keep it in place. Align the bottom of the rafters with the marks on the double top plate. Attach them with 16-penny nails. Add the end rafters at the opposite end. Then continue adding rafters until the roof framing is complete.

18 Add Fascia

Once the rafters are in place, you can add the fascia. Fascia covers the ends of the rafters to protect them and provide a more finished look; a common fascia material is 1 × 4 or 1 × 6 primed pine. Depending on your shed plans, you may want to cover the end rafters with fascia as well. If so, cut these to length now and attach them with 8-penny galvanized finish nails. You can butt the ends of the fascia together at the corners as shown or miter

thicker sheathing offers. In preparation for the asphalt shingles apply 15-pound roofing felt. This type of roofing (shown on page 24) is easy to apply, inexpensive, and will last for years. (See page 113 for alternative roofing choices.) Exterior-grade ⅝-inch-thick tongue-and-groove sheathing is an excellent choice for most roofs. Start at the bottom and work your way to the top, making sure the end of each panel falls over the center of a rafter; trim if necessary. Also, make sure that

them. Secure the fascia to each rafter end with two 8-penny galvanized nails.

19 Attach Sheathing

Once the roof framing is in place, you can add the roof sheathing. The thickness and type of sheathing you use will depend on local codes. Even if code allows for thin sheathing, avoid anything less than ½ inch thick, as this doesn't provide as solid a nailing base as

you stagger the panels so the joints don't align. Leave a ⅛-inch expansion gap between panels, and secure them to the rafters with 8-penny roofing nails every 6 inches or so. Add panels until the entire roof is sheathed.

20 Attach Roofing Felt

Adding a layer of roofing felt (also called tar paper) on top of the sheathing and fascia protects the roofing from moisture. To align

the rows of roofing felt, measure 33⅝ inches above the eaves and snap a chalk line. Then, allowing for a 2-inch overlap between the strips, snap each succeeding line at 34 inches. Start applying strips from the bottom up, taking care to align them with the chalk lines. Where two strips meet at a vertical line, overlap them at least 4 inches. Use only enough staples or nails to hold the felt in place until the shingles can be installed.

21 Add Drip Edge

Before adding the asphalt shingles, protect the edges of the roof with drip edge. Drip edge is malleable aluminum that's preformed into a right angle with a slight lip along one edge to help direct water runoff away from the fascia and exterior siding. Cut a 45-degree miter at each end with metal snips. Press the drip edge in place so it butts firmly up against the fascia, and secure it every 12 inches or so with roofing nails.

22 Install Shingles

Asphalt shingles use a self-sealing mastic to fasten the shingles together once they're heated by the sun (for more on asphalt shingles, see page 113). In order for the first course of shingles to fasten to the front edge of the roof, a special starter row is first installed. The starter row is 7-inch strips cut from full shingles and installed upside down along the eaves to position the mastic near the edge, where it will stick to the first full row installed. Secure the starter row with roofing nails 3 inches above the eaves. Install the first course of shingles, allowing ½-inch overhang. Snap a chalk line 10 inches up from the bottom of the first course, and install the second course, offsetting horizontally by a half tab. Continue snapping reference lines and adding courses until you reach the ridge.

23 Attach the Ridge Cap

Use ready-made ridge shingles or cut your own 12-inch squares from standard shingles. On the most visible side of the shed, snap a line parallel to and 6 inches down from the ridge. Starting at the end opposite the prevailing wind, apply the shingles, leaving a 5-inch exposure; align the edges with the chalk marks. Nail on each side, 5½ inches from the butt and 1 inch from the outside edge.

24 Install Exterior Siding

Plywood siding is the least expensive and easiest to install siding for a shed. T1-11 exterior tongue-and-groove siding is a good choice; for other siding alternatives, see page 102. Start by positioning the first sheet vertically at one corner so its edge is flush with the corner framing. Check that the opposite edge reaches the center of a wall stud; shift the panel and trim as necessary. Attach the siding to the wall studs using 8-penny galvanized finish nails every 6 inches around the perimeter and every 12 inches elsewhere. Install the remaining sheets, leaving an ⅛-inch expansion gap between sheets. When possible, apply siding over window and door openings, then cut out the siding with a saber or reciprocating saw.

25 Add Windows and Doors

Position the prehung window or door in the rough opening and insert pairs of shims around the perimeter. Adjust the shims as necessary to make the unit plumb and level. To secure the window or door, drive galvanized casing nails through the jamb and shims and into the jack studs, sill (if applicable), and header. Trim off any protruding shims. Secure windows with nailing flanges or pre-installed brick molding to the exterior siding, using galvanized nails driven through the siding and into the framing.

26 Finish Off with Trim

All that's left to complete your shed is to install trim around windows and doors, and along the top and/or bottom of the exterior walls if desired. Just make sure to use galvanized finish nails; pre-primed trim is available that makes painting your trim a quick and easy task. Trim can be minimal or fanciful; for examples of what you can do with trim, see pages 18–19. For more on working with trim, see page 109.

gambrel shed

For serious storage space and lots of headroom, consider this gambrel-roof storage shed. At 12 feet by 16 feet, it will not only shelter mowers, motorcycles, and other sizable items, but also offer overhead storage. Planks laid across the ceiling joists can add even more usable space to this flexible design.

This roomy shed has a ramp and generous double doors that make the ins and outs of storage easy. Concrete pier footings support the structure, though it can also be built on a slab. (To purchase this shed in kit form, see page 160.)

DESIGN: KEVIN DOWN, NORTHERN PINE SHEDS.

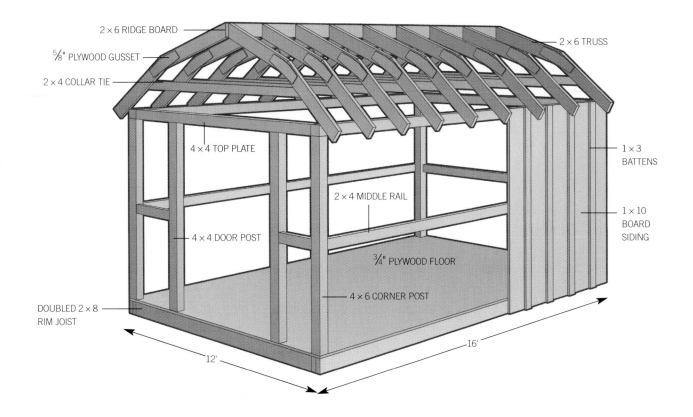

2 × 6 RIDGE BOARD

⅝" PLYWOOD GUSSET

2 × 4 COLLAR TIE

2 × 6 TRUSS

4 × 4 TOP PLATE

1 × 3 BATTENS

2 × 4 MIDDLE RAIL

4 × 4 DOOR POST

1 × 10 BOARD SIDING

¾" PLYWOOD FLOOR

4 × 6 CORNER POST

DOUBLED 2 × 8 RIM JOIST

16'

12'

DESIGN DETAILS

Reminiscent of a timber-framed barn, this eminently practical gambrel shed uses many of the same construction principles. The 4 × 6 corner posts support 4 × 4 top plates and door posts. Wall studs aren't required, since the board-and-batten siding (attached to the top plate, middle rail, and framed floor) serves to bear the weight of the roof.

The gambrel roof is framed by making rafter-like truss sections that attach to the ridge board. Collar ties span the truss sections to create a sturdy roof. If desired, you can place windows above the middle rail by cutting an opening in the siding and attaching a flanged window.

MATERIALS LIST

NAME	DIMENSIONS
Concrete and pea gravel for footings	
Floor joists	2 × 8
Tongue-and-groove plywood flooring	¾-inch
Corner posts	4 × 6
Top plates and door posts	4 × 4
Middle rails and collar ties	2 × 4
Rough-sawn siding	1 × 10
Siding battens	1 × 3
Rafters	2 × 6
Ridge board	2 × 6
Plywood roof sheathing and gussets	⅝-inch
Fascia	1 × 6
Drip edge and 15-lb. roofing felt	
Asphalt shingles	
Galvanized nails and outdoor screws	
Metal post anchors	
Metal framing brackets and fasteners	
Strap hinges and door latch	
Paint, stain, or wood preservative	

HOW TO BUILD A GAMBREL SHED

The large size of this shed requires poured footings (see pages 99–100) or a reinforced concrete slab. If you choose a slab, you won't need to build the framed floor described in Step 1 below. Also, although the door posts and top plates call for 4 × 4 beams, you can safely substitute 2 × 4s nailed together every 6 inches or so. The 1 × 10 siding is key to the strength of this structure: Do not substitute other siding materials.

1 Frame the Floor

The outside frame pieces (technically known as rim joists) for the floor are made up of doubled pressure-treated pine 2 × 8s. The side pieces are 16 feet long and the ends are 11 feet 6 inches to make a true 12-foot × 16-foot frame. Join the frame pieces with 16d nails and L-brackets on the inside corners. For the internal joists, cut pressure-treated 2 × 8s to 11 feet 6 inches and attach them to the frame with joist hangers (page 102), 24 inches on center (see pages 101 and 104). Set the completed frame on the footings and secure it to the metal post

anchors (see page 100). Cover the frame with ¾-inch tongue-and-groove plywood, using 8d nails or 2-inch galvanized deck screws.

2 Build the Walls

Cut four 4 × 6 corner posts 7 feet long for the front wall. Cut the top plates (see page 101) to length to rest on the corner posts while leaving 3½ inches for the top plate of the side wall. Position the door posts according to the width of door you want. Lay the top plates and posts on the floor and attach them by toenailing 16d nails or using metal angle brackets. Build the rear wall.

With a helper, tip the front and back walls into position and attach the posts to the floor with 16d galvanized nails (no bottom plates are required).

3 Level and Plumb the Walls

Level and plumb the walls and add temporary diagonal bracing inside the shed from post to post to keep each square. To hold the wall upright and plumb, add 4-foot-long temporary braces reaching from the rim joist to midway up each corner post. Cut and attach the 2 × 4 middle rail 36 inches up from the floor. Recheck each wall for plumb.

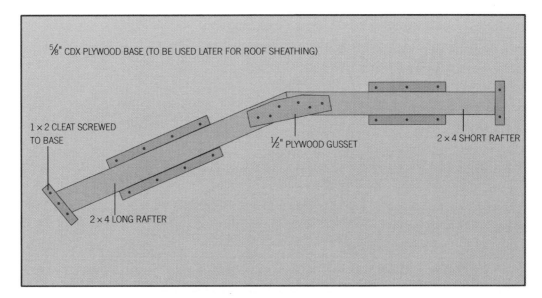

⅝" CDX PLYWOOD BASE (TO BE USED LATER FOR ROOF SHEATHING)

1 × 2 CLEAT SCREWED TO BASE

½" PLYWOOD GUSSET

2 × 4 SHORT RAFTER

2 × 4 LONG RAFTER

TRUSS SECTION ASSEMBLY JIG

COMPLETED TRUSS

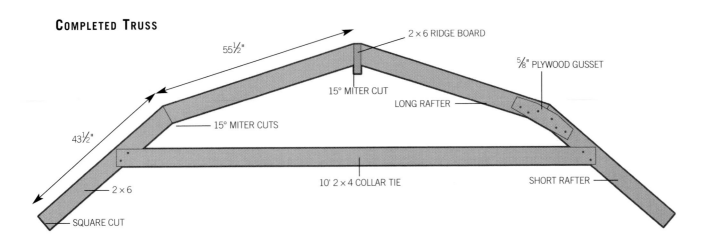

2 × 6 RIDGE BOARD

55½"

⅝" PLYWOOD GUSSET

15° MITER CUT

LONG RAFTER

43½"

15° MITER CUTS

10' 2 × 4 COLLAR TIE

SHORT RAFTER

2 × 6

SQUARE CUT

4 Add the Top Plates

Cut the side top plates long enough to overlap the top of each 4 × 6 corner post. Clamp or tack the top plates together, and lay out the rafter locations 24 inches on center (see page 104); do this to the 2 × 6 ridge board as well. Attach the top plates. Cut and attach the middle rails to the posts. Attach temporary 1 × 4 diagonal supports to the inside of the walls to keep them from racking. Recheck the entire structure for plumb and level, and adjust as necessary.

5 Add the Siding

Enclose the wall frame by cutting 1 × 10 siding boards to 93½ inches for the eaves sides and attaching them flush with the top plate. Then cover the siding seams with 1 × 3s cut to the same length.

6 Install the Gable Boards

Next, cut 1 × 10 gable siding boards 12 feet long so they'll run "wild" on top (they will be trimmed to length after the rafters are up). Cover the gable siding seams with battens, once again letting them run wild on top.

7 Frame the Roof

Start the roof by temporarily attaching the ridge board that you laid out earlier to the gable siding so it's centered 11 feet 6 inches up from the floor. Then cut pairs of short and long rafters as shown above. Make the truss section assembly jig (shown opposite) and then fabricate each side of the truss by attaching ⅝-inch plywood gussets to the pairs of rafters, using 8d nails or 2-inch screws.

8 Cut the Gable

Hold a truss section up against the inside of the ridge board gable siding and mark the outline on the siding; cut to the marked line with a circular saw or reciprocating saw and repeat for the opposite end. Attach the end trusses to the ridge board, top plate, and siding. Nail the remaining rafter pairs to the ridge board and secure them to the top plates with sheet-metal fasteners known as hurricane ties. Connect the truss sections with 10-foot-long collar ties, using 16d nails. Then cut and attach 1 × 6 fascia to the ends of the rafters.

9 Finish the Roof

Cover the roof frame with ⅝-inch CDX plywood sheathing, starting at the bottom and working up toward the ridge (see page 115). Add drip edge and 15-pound roofing felt. Install asphalt shingles and ridge caps (consult pages 113–115 for how to apply asphalt and other types of shingles).

10 Add the Door

Build a door to fit the opening (see the detail drawing on page 53). Attach the door to the frame with strap hinges, and add the door latch. If desired, attach screening between the ends of the rafters and the top plates to keep out insects. Cut and attach corner trim and door trim.

small gable shed

No question why this is the most popular shed style: Its clean gable roof design fits almost any setting, and the full-height door opens on simple, functional space to suit multiple needs. Whether a storage building, children's playhouse, mini-office, or poolside cabana, this shed is number one.

Second only to a lean-to shed (pages 58–61), a gable shed like this is wonderfully simple to build. Add shutters, window boxes, and a Dutch door, vary the siding a bit, and you have a nicely detailed project that belies its uncomplicated origins. (To purchase this shed in kit form, see Resources, page 160.)

DESIGN: SUMMERWOOD INDUSTRIES.

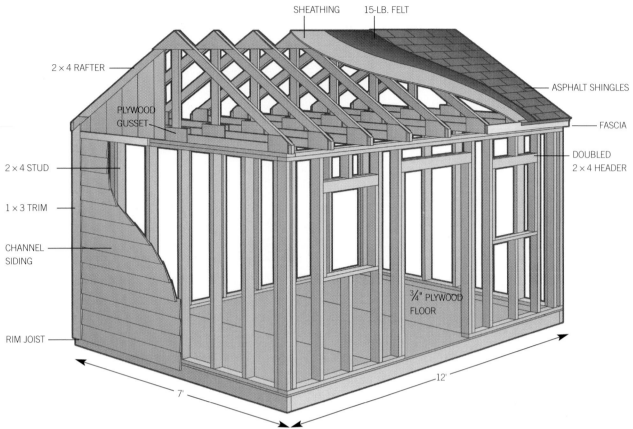

SHEATHING   15-LB. FELT

2 × 4 RAFTER

PLYWOOD GUSSET

2 × 4 STUD

1 × 3 TRIM

CHANNEL SIDING

RIM JOIST

ASPHALT SHINGLES

FASCIA

DOUBLED 2 × 4 HEADER

¾" PLYWOOD FLOOR

7'

12'

DESIGN DETAILS

Because of its diminutive size, this gable shed doesn't require a heavy-duty foundation; it can rest on skids or precast concrete piers (or for added stability, poured footings). The simple design is easy to enlarge or reduce. The 7 × 12-foot shed shown here can easily be shortened, leaving just a single window and a door in front (see photo opposite).

The gable roof is built with simple king-post trusses, which simplify construction and make for a very solid structure. The roof frame can be covered with plywood sheathing and asphalt shingles (see pages 113 and 115), or battens and cedar shingles (see page 113).

MATERIALS LIST

NAME	DIMENSIONS
Pressure-treated skids, concrete piers, or concrete and pea gravel for footings	
Floor joists	2 × 4
Pressure-treated runners	2 × 6
Tongue-and-groove plywood flooring	¾-inch
Top/bottom plates and wall studs	2 × 4
Ceiling joists, rafters, and truss supports	2 × 4
Plywood gussets	⅝-inch
CDX roof sheathing	⅝-inch
4-light windows	2' 0" x 2' 4"
Cedar channel siding	1 × 6
Cedar shutter trim	1 × 2
Cedar soffits, fascia, end caps, and window boxes	1 × 6
Cedar corner trim, door and window trim	1 × 3
Cedar door boards, threshold, and casing	1 × 6
Drip edge and 15-lb. roofing felt	
Asphalt shingles and ridge caps	
Galvanized nails and outdoor screws	
Anchor bolts	
Metal framing brackets and fasteners	
Strap hinges and door latch	
Paint, stain, or wood preservative	

HOW TO BUILD A GABLE SHED

If you're planning on using skids for a foundation, cut three 7-foot-long 4 × 6 pressure-treated beams. Center one under the shed, and position the other two 36 inches to each side of it. Precast concrete piers or poured footings should be set in 6 inches along the front and back sides of the shed and spaced 36 inches apart. Along the length of the shed set them in 16 inches and space them 56 inches apart. Span the piers or footings with 12-foot pressure-treated 2 × 6s and attach them with anchor bolts.

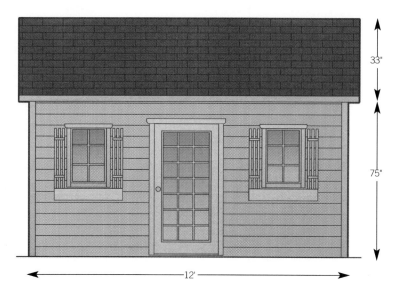

1 Frame the Floor

Build the floor frame by first cutting rim joists 84 inches long. Lay out the floor joists on these, 16 inches on center, and cut the floor joists 141 inches long. Attach these to the rim joists with 16d nails or joist hangers. Position the frame on the runners and shim them level. Check the diagonals, and when square, toenail the frame to the runners. Cover the framing with plywood sheathing.

2 Build Walls

To build each wall section, first cut matching top and bottom plates to length. Then lay out the wall studs and rough openings. Cut enough wall studs 72 inches long for 16 inches on-center spacing, and assemble each wall.

Frame rough openings by adding jack studs, headers, cripple studs, and sills as required.

3 Raise the Walls

Raise the walls by setting the first wall on the floor and secure it by driving 3-inch screws through the bottom plate into the floor frame. Brace the wall temporarily and raise the remaining wall sections. Check for plumb, and secure the walls to each other at the corners.

Cut the double top plates, but before attaching them to the walls, lay out truss locations 24 inches on center. Install the double top plates, then cut out the bottom plate at the door opening.

4 Frame the Roof

The roof is framed with trusses; each is made of a 96-inch-long ceiling joist, two 50-inch-long rafters mitered on the ends, and

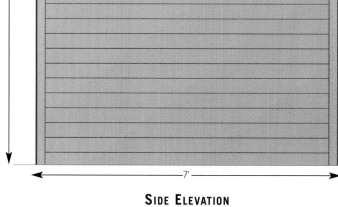

SIDE ELEVATION

7-IN-12 SLOPE

33"

75"

7'

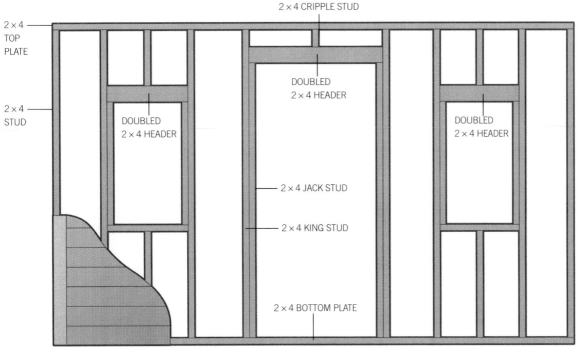

WALL SECTION

Labels on diagram:
- 2 × 4 CRIPPLE STUD
- 2 × 4 TOP PLATE
- 2 × 4 STUD
- DOUBLED 2 × 4 HEADER
- DOUBLED 2 × 4 HEADER
- DOUBLED 2 × 4 HEADER
- 2 × 4 JACK STUD
- 2 × 4 KING STUD
- 2 × 4 BOTTOM PLATE

a 21-inch-long truss support mitered to fit under the rafters. The truss parts are joined with ⅝-inch plywood gussets as shown in the truss detail below. You'll need seven trusses for the 12-foot-long shed described here; trusses are 24 inches on center.

5 Attach Trusses

Once the trusses are assembled, attach the end trusses to the double top plates so they're flush with the side of the wall frame and the eaves overhang is even. Temporarily span the two end trusses with a 2 × 4 to serve as a positioning guide; position the remaining trusses on the marks made earlier on the double top plates, and toenail them in place.

6 Finish the Roof

Cover the trusses with ⅝-inch CDX plywood sheathing, starting at the bottom and working up toward the ridge. Add drip edge and 15-pound roofing felt. Install asphalt shingles and ridge caps.

7 Enclose the Walls

To enclose the walls, cut and install cedar channel siding horizontally, starting from the bottom and working to the top plate. (Note: If you're using windows with flanged trim, install them before the siding.) Allow the bottom edge of the first piece to overhang the bottom plate by ¼ inch. On the gable ends, cut and attach the siding vertically once you've reached the top plate. Cut and install the soffits, fascia, and corner trim.

8 Install Windows and Doors

Install windows in rough openings, and trim them with 1 × 3 cedar. Install a prehung door or build a board-and-batten door to fit the rough opening, and attach it with strap hinges and a door latch. Trim around the windows, and add shutter trim if desired.

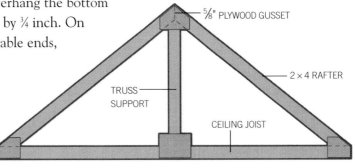

Labels on truss detail:
- ⅝" PLYWOOD GUSSET
- 2 × 4 RAFTER
- TRUSS SUPPORT
- CEILING JOIST

TRUSS DETAIL

gable shed with porch

The sheltering porch makes this twist on the classic gable style both attractive and versatile. At roughly 8 feet by 12 feet, including the 4-foot porch, this model is ideal for storage, a workshop, barbecues, or just relaxing. The shed features a front slide-down porch window that makes it ideal for entertaining.

While the detailing of the porch makes this shed slightly more challenging than some, it remains an essentially simple project. In fact, it's a great shed for practicing some carpentry skills and trying a few variations on the basic gable-shed theme. (To purchase this shed in kit form, see page 160.)

DESIGN: CEDARSHED INDUSTRIES, INC.

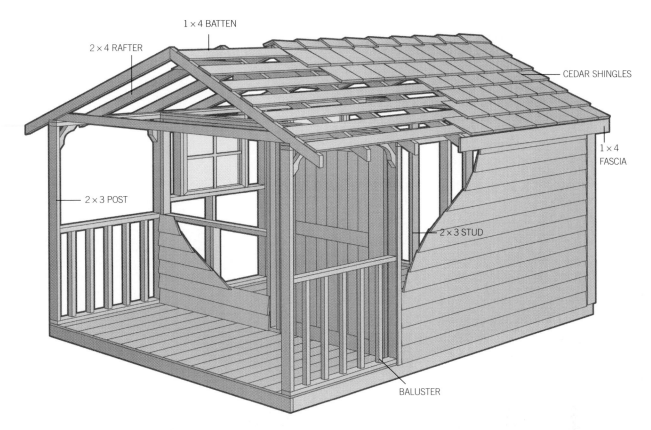

1 × 4 BATTEN

2 × 4 RAFTER

CEDAR SHINGLES

1 × 4 FASCIA

2 × 3 POST

2 × 3 STUD

BALUSTER

DESIGN DETAILS

Although this stick-framed design calls for 2 × 3 framing components, you may want to use conventional 2 × 4s—they are stronger and are easier to buy. If you do, be sure to compensate for the added width as you build.

A large single-pane window in front slides up and down on a simple wood track. A pair of wood blocks are screwed to the bottom of the track to serve as stops. Handrail and balusters partially enclose the porch. For a custom touch, design your own brackets or use wooden shelf brackets (if you do this, be sure to beef up the fasteners, and stain and seal them for outdoor use).

MATERIALS LIST

NAME	DIMENSIONS
Pea gravel and precast concrete piers or concrete for footings	
Floor joists	2 × 3 or 2 × 4
Tongue-and-groove plywood flooring or	¾-inch
cedar tongue-and-groove flooring	1 × 4
Top/bottom plates and wall studs	2 × 3 or 2 × 4
Double top plates	1 × 3 or 1 × 4
Ceiling joists, rafters, and collar ties	2 × 3 or 2 × 4
Open sheathing (battens)	1 × 4
Cedar roofing shingles and ridge caps	
Cedar bevel siding	½ × 6
Cedar top and skirting	½ × 3
Cedar corner trim and bottom skirting	1 × 4
Soffits	½ × 4
Fascia	1 × 4
Cedar trim	1 × 2
Balusters	2 × 2
4-light windows	2' 0" × 2' 4"
1-light window	3' 6" × 2' 6"
Galvanized nails and outdoor screws	
Metal post anchors, framing brackets, and fasteners	
Door hinges and door set	
Paint, stain, or wood preservative	

HOW TO BUILD A GABLE SHED WITH PORCH

This shed can be built on skids, precast concrete piers, or footings. If you pour a slab foundation, the joists and flooring are optional—you can attach the bottom plates of the walls directly to the slab. The roof battens are necessary only for wood shingles or shakes. For asphalt shingles, substitute ⅝-inch plywood sheathing and add drip edge to overlap the fascia.

1 Frame the Floor

The framed floor rests on concrete piers or poured footings spaced approximately every 4 feet. To build the frame, lay out joists on two 12-foot rim joists 16 inches on center. Then cut 12 floor joists 90 inches long and attach them to the rim joists with nails or joist hangers (see page 102). Position the frame on the piers or footings and level it with shims. Cover the framing with tongue-and-groove pine or cedar flooring (as shown) or ¼-inch plywood sheathing.

2 Construct the Walls

Begin making the walls by cutting eight 93-inch top and bottom plates for all four walls. Lay out the wall studs (pages 101 and 104) at 24 inches on center for the rear wall and one side wall; lay out rough openings for windows and door on the front wall and the remaining side wall. Cut wall studs as needed to 71⅜ inches, and assemble each wall section. Add sills, headers, and cripple studs as required (see pages 101–105 for more on framing).

3 Raise and Brace the Walls

Position the rear wall flush with the floor; screw it to the flooring, bracing as needed. Repeat this for the side and front walls. Check for level and plumb and screw the

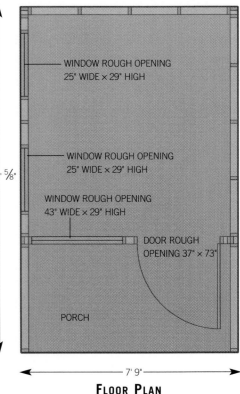

WINDOW ROUGH OPENING
25" WIDE × 29" HIGH

WINDOW ROUGH OPENING
25" WIDE × 29" HIGH

WINDOW ROUGH OPENING
43" WIDE × 29" HIGH

DOOR ROUGH
OPENING 37" × 73"

PORCH

12' 5⁄8"

7' 9"

FLOOR PLAN

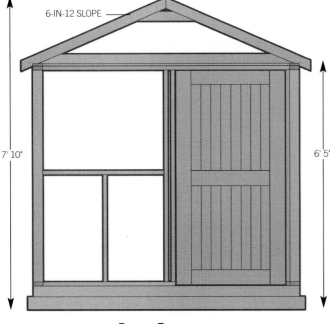

6-IN-12 SLOPE

7' 10"

6' 5"

FRONT ELEVATION

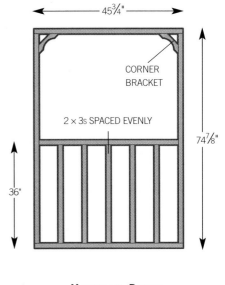

45¾"

CORNER
BRACKET

2 × 3s SPACED EVENLY

36"

74⅞"

HANDRAIL DETAIL

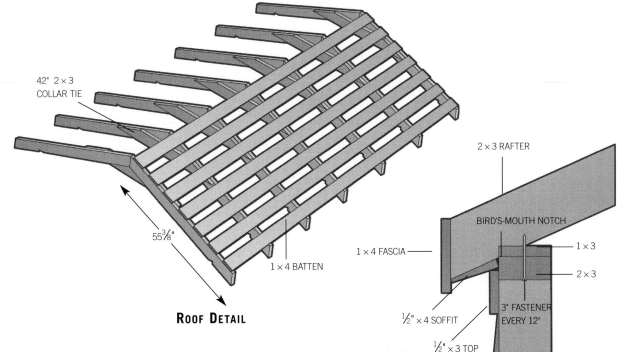

42" 2 × 3
COLLAR TIE

55 $\frac{3}{8}$"

1 × 4 BATTEN

Roof Detail

2 × 3 RAFTER

BIRD'S-MOUTH NOTCH

1 × 4 FASCIA

1 × 3

2 × 3

½" × 4 SOFFIT

3" FASTENER
EVERY 12"

½" × 3 TOP
SKIRTING

SIDING

Rafter Detail

wall sections together at the corners. Before you attach the 1 × 3 double top plates, lay out rafter locations 24 inches on center. Cut parts for the handrail partitions and assemble them; position and fasten them to the floor frame.

4 Fabricate the Trusses

The roof slope is 6 in 12, framed with trusses. Cut the rafters to length (see the roof detail), and cut the bird's-mouth notches (see rafter detail). Connect pairs of rafters with 42-inch-long collar ties; toenail at the ridge. Position the trusses on the double top plates and attach them by screwing up through the top plates and into the rafters (two trusses go on top of the handrail partition).

5 Add the Roofing

To cover the trusses with cedar shingles, start by installing 1 × 4 open sheathing (battens) on both sides of the ridge to keep the trusses spaced at 24 inches on center. Install the remaining open sheathing, spacing apart for the desired shingle exposure. Starting at the bottom, attach shingles to 1 × 4 battens and work toward the top. Install cap shingles along the ridge. (See pages 113–115 for more on roofing.)

6 Add the Windows and Door

Install side windows in the rough openings. The front window rides in a 2 × 2 track fastened to the inside of the wall. To keep the window from sliding down onto the floor when open, screw a pair of scrap stops to the track to stop the window in the fully opened position. Build a door to fit the opening; mount with door hinges. Install a door set if desired.

7 Siding and Finishing Touches

Enclose the walls with ½-inch × 6-inch bevel siding. Start at the bottom and work up, using a 1-inch overlap and fastening the siding to the studs with 6d galvanized nails. (See page 105 for more on siding.) Cut and install window trim, door trim, and shutter trim as desired. Final trim includes corner trim, 1 × 4 fascia on the ends of rafters, and ½-inch × 4-inch soffits, along with top and bottom skirting.

gable shed with storage bay

From the front, this simple shed design doesn't reveal its "secret": a rear, covered storage bay that offers multiple uses. Use it to store more than a cord of firewood, or make the entire bay a protected area for a potting bench or workbench.

Slightly more challenging to build than the gable shed on pages 38–41, this shed has a more complex eaves treatment and includes a sheltered storage (see page 24) supported by a doubled beam. Still, this is a straightforward design that can be built in a few weekends. (To purchase plans for this project, see page 160.)
DESIGN: GARLINGHOUSE COMPANY.

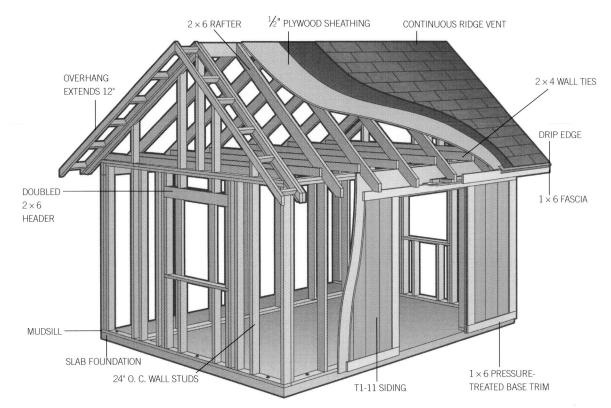

2 × 6 RAFTER
½" PLYWOOD SHEATHING
CONTINUOUS RIDGE VENT
OVERHANG EXTENDS 12"
2 × 4 WALL TIES
DRIP EDGE
DOUBLED 2 × 6 HEADER
1 × 6 FASCIA
MUDSILL
SLAB FOUNDATION
24" O. C. WALL STUDS
T1-11 SIDING
1 × 6 PRESSURE-TREATED BASE TRIM

DESIGN DETAILS

This 8-foot by 12-foot stick-framed shed is designed to be built on a slab foundation, but can also be erected on poured footings and a framed floor, as shown for the Saltbox shed described on page 52.

The highly sloped roof (a 12-in-12 pitch) sheds water and snow well, and the eaves extend out to shield the gable siding from the weather.

T1-11 siding is shown, but with the addition of ½-inch CDX plywood wall sheathing you could add board-and-batten or lap siding (see pages 102 and 105 for more on siding options and techniques).

MATERIALS LIST

NAME	DIMENSIONS
Crushed stone	
vapor retarder	6 mil
Rebar	#5
Wire mesh	6 × 6
Concrete	
Pressure-treated mudsills	2 × 4
Wall studs, top/double top plates, wall ties, gable studs, eaves framing	2 × 4
Beams and ridge board	2 × 8
Headers and rafters	2 × 6
Siding	⅝" T1-11
Soffit nailer	2 × 2
CDX roof sheathing	½" × 4 × 8
Trim, fascia, frieze board	1 × 6
Ridge vent, drip edge, roofing felt	
Asphalt shingles	
Windows	3' 0" × 3' 0"
Double door	4' 0" × 6' 8"
Galvanized nails and outdoor screws	
Anchor bolts	
Metal framing brackets and fasteners	
Door hinges and door set	
Paint, stain, or wood preservative	

HOW TO BUILD A GABLE SHED WITH STORAGE BAY

Be sure to study the step-by-step photography illustrating the construction of this shed on pages 24–33. Adding the overhang at the gables and trimming out the soffit at the eaves are the most challenging aspects of this project. In addition, you'll have the opportunity to cut a true rafter, bird's mouth and all. Expect this to be a trial-and-error process until you get two rafters that fit just right.

1 Pour the Slab

The slab foundation shown here uses rebar and welded wire mesh for reinforcement (see foundation detail below). Along the width of the slab, press anchor bolts into the wet concrete 2 inches in from the edges. Place anchors 6 inches in from the corners and centered along the width of the slab. Along the length of the door side of the slab, place anchors 9 inches in from each corner with one central anchor 6 inches from the door opening. Also add an anchor 11 inches in from the edge to hold the storage central partition wall.

2 Build the Walls

Cut pressure-treated 2 × 4 mudsills to length, mark the anchor locations, and drill holes. Cut top plates to length and lay out wall studs (see pages 101 and 104) 24 inches on center on pairs of mudsills and top plates (see floor plan for dimensions). Lay out the rough openings, and cut and assemble headers. Build each wall, adding jack studs, sills, headers, and cripple studs as needed.

3 Raise the Walls

Lift each wall so that the mudsill fits over the anchor bolts. Place washers over the bolts, and thread on nuts but do not fully tighten. Brace each wall as necessary. Check the walls for level and plumb, nail the walls together at the corners, and tighten the nuts on the mudsills. Cut and install the double top plates; cut the bottom plate at the door opening.

4 Frame the Roof

The roof is framed using ceiling joists, rafters, and a ridge board. Make a rafter template, using the pattern shown below; then cut the rafters to size. Next, lay out the ridge board for 24-inch on-center rafters, and transfer these locations to the double top plates (see page 104). Attach a pair of rafters to each end of the ridge board, and lift this up onto the double top plates. Cut a center

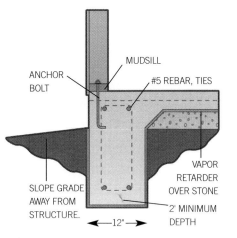

ANCHOR BOLT

MUDSILL

#5 REBAR, TIES

VAPOR RETARDER OVER STONE

SLOPE GRADE AWAY FROM STRUCTURE.

2' MINIMUM DEPTH

←12'→

FOUNDATION DETAIL

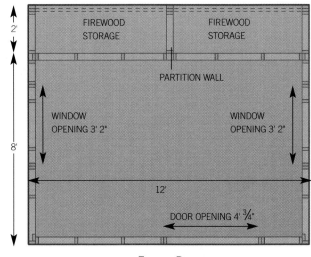

2'

8'

FIREWOOD STORAGE

FIREWOOD STORAGE

PARTITION WALL

WINDOW OPENING 3' 2"

WINDOW OPENING 3' 2"

12'

DOOR OPENING 4' $\frac{3}{4}$"

FLOOR PLAN

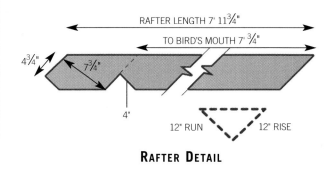

RAFTER LENGTH 7' 11$\frac{3}{4}$"

TO BIRD'S MOUTH 7' $\frac{3}{4}$"

4$\frac{3}{4}$"

7$\frac{3}{4}$"

4"

12" RUN   12" RISE

RAFTER DETAIL

gable stud and toenail it in place; repeat for the opposite end. Install the other rafters. Then cut and install the gable overhang framing (these pieces are cut much like rafters); this "ladder" is then attached to the end rafters.

5 Frame the Gable End
Cut gable studs to fit directly above the wall studs. Use a level to align each gable stud and then mark and cut the angle. Toenail the gable studs in place. Cut and install the wall ties.

6 Enclose the Shed
Cut sheets of T1-11 siding to fit so that the edges are always centered on studs. Attach the siding to the studs with galvanized 8d nails every 8 inches or so. Cover the roof framing with ½-inch CDX plywood sheathing.

7 Add the Trim
Before shingling the roof, it's best to add the fascia and trim (see rafter and eaves detail right). Cut and install the eaves fascia, a 2 × 2 continuous soffit nailer, and 2 × 2 framing between the continuous nailer and each rafter tail. Cut and install the soffit vent and the ⅜-inch plywood soffit. Add the 1 × 6 rake trim and the soffit under the gable overhangs.

8 Apply the Roofing
Attach 15-pound roofing felt and install drip edge along the gables and eaves. Install the continuous

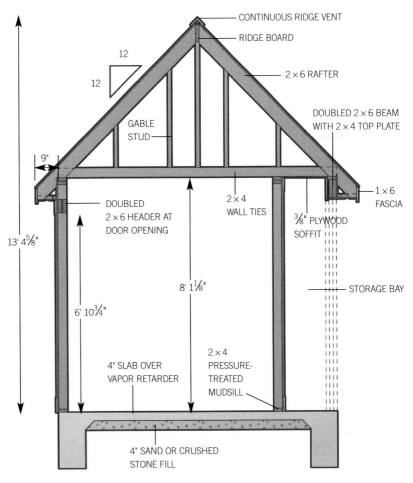

SIDE VIEW SECTION

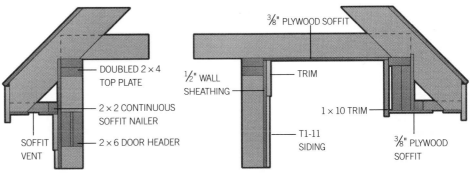

RAFTER AND EAVES DETAIL

ridge vent, then attach the shingles and ridge cap. (See pages 113 and 115 for more on roofing.)

9 Install the Door and Windows
Shim for level and plumb and attach doors and windows with galvanized casing nails. (If double

doors are unavailable, make them from ¾-inch exterior plywood and 2 × 2s.) Cut and attach base trim, corner boards, 1 × 6 frieze board (the horizontal trim on each gable side), and window trim. Finally, cut and install corner boards, beam trim, and soffit returns.

saltbox shed

The major benefit of this classic design is headroom: Almost as soon as you enter, you can stand straight up to use the ample space inside. Board-and-batten siding on this 8-by-12-foot saltbox contributes to the visual symmetry and simple lines that make it enormously popular.

For a truly rural silhouette, consider the attractive simplicity of a saltbox shed. This example includes a ramp and ample double doors for stowing lawn and garden equipment. With minor modifications—a Dutch door and larger windows—this salt-box could easily be a potting shed. (To buy this shed in kit form, see page 160.)

DESIGN: KEVIN DOWN, NORTHERN PINE SHEDS.

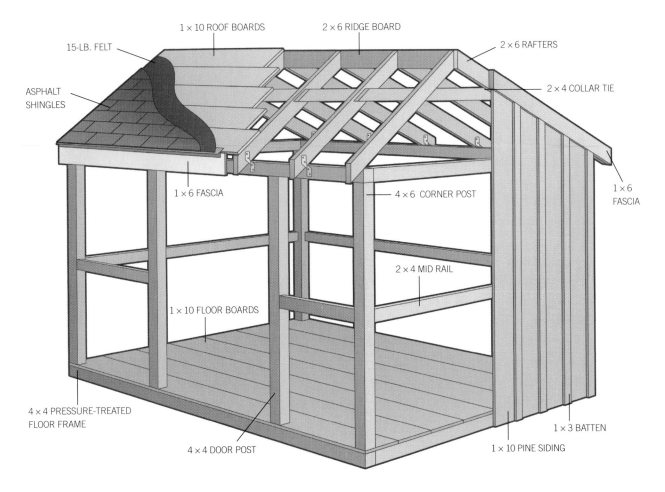

15-LB. FELT

ASPHALT SHINGLES

1 × 10 ROOF BOARDS

2 × 6 RIDGE BOARD

2 × 6 RAFTERS

2 × 4 COLLAR TIE

1 × 6 FASCIA

1 × 6 FASCIA

4 × 6 CORNER POST

2 × 4 MID RAIL

1 × 10 FLOOR BOARDS

4 × 4 PRESSURE-TREATED FLOOR FRAME

4 × 4 DOOR POST

1 × 3 BATTEN

1 × 10 PINE SIDING

DESIGN DETAILS

Designed to stand up to the toughest weather, this stout saltbox shed uses timber-framing techniques (often called post-and-beam construction). But don't worry, there's no fancy mortise-and-tenon joinery needed here—the large beams are simply nailed together. The strength comes from attaching 1 × 10 board-and-batten siding to the beams to create a surprisingly rigid structure.

The offset ridge roof is stick-framed using rafters, a ridge board, and collar ties. You can place windows anywhere above the middle rail by cutting openings in the siding and attaching flanged windows.

MATERIALS LIST

NAME	DIMENSIONS
Concrete and pea gravel for footings	
Pressure-treated beams for floor frame	4 × 4
Flooring	1 × 10
Corner posts	4 × 6
Top plates and door posts	4 × 4
Middle rails and collar ties	2 × 4
Siding boards	1 × 10
Siding battens	1 × 3
Ridge board and rafters	2 × 6
Roof boards	1 × 10
Drip edge and 15-lb. roofing felt	
Asphalt shingles	
Sliding windows	2' 0" x 2' 0"
Fascia	1 × 6
Trim	1 × 3
Galvanized nails and outdoor screws	
Metal post anchors	
Metal framing brackets and fasteners	
Strap hinges and door latch	
Paint, stain, or wood preservative	

HOW TO BUILD A SALTBOX SHED

This 8-foot by 12-foot shed can be built on skids, concrete piers, or poured footings. Although this design calls for double doors, it can easily be modified for a single door. Also, because of the post-and-beam construction, you can install as many windows as you like on any or all sides of the shed. Note that although the door posts and top plates call for 4 × 4 beams, you can safely substitute 2 × 4s nailed together every 6 inches or so. The 1 × 10 siding is key to the strength of this structure: Do not substitute other siding materials.

1 Install the Foundation

The foundation for this shed can be skids, concrete piers, or poured footings (see pages 98–99). The floor frame is 4 × 4 pressure-treated pine; the long pieces are 12 feet long, and the ends and joists are 7 feet 5 inches long. Together they make an 8-foot by 12-foot frame.

Connect the frame by toenailing parts together, or use joist hangers; joists are 24 inches on center (see pages 26–27 and 101 for how to lay these out). Place the completed frame on the footings, shim the frame level, and secure it to the footings. To cover the frame, cut 8-foot-long 1 × 10s and use 8d nails to secure them to the frame (alternatively, use ¾-inch tongue-and-groove plywood).

2 Build the Walls

Cut four 4 × 6 corner posts 6 feet 3 inches long, and secure these with nails (no bottom plates are required). Cut the top plates to length to rest on the corner posts. Before attaching the long top plates, lay out the rafter locations 24 inches on center; do this to the 12-foot-long 2 × 6 ridge board as well. Cut and install the 4 × 4 door posts.

Level and plumb the walls and add temporary diagonal bracing inside the shed from post to post to keep it square. Cut and attach the 2 × 4 middle rail 36 inches up from the floor.

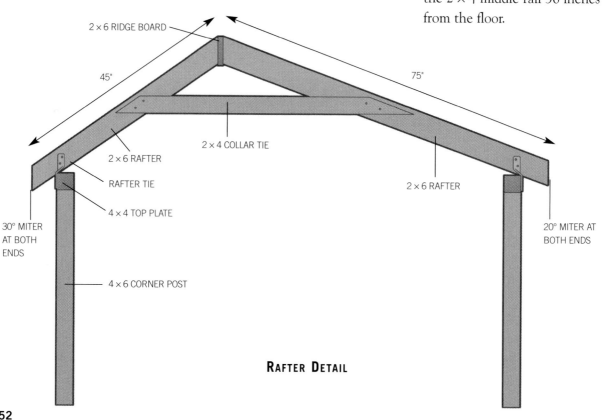

2 × 6 RIDGE BOARD

45"

75"

2 × 4 COLLAR TIE

2 × 6 RAFTER

RAFTER TIE

2 × 6 RAFTER

4 × 4 TOP PLATE

30° MITER AT BOTH ENDS

20° MITER AT BOTH ENDS

4 × 6 CORNER POST

RAFTER DETAIL

3 Enclose the Wall Frame

Cut 1 × 10 siding boards to 81½ inches for the eave sides and attach them flush with the top plate. Then cover the siding seams with 1 × 3s cut to the same length. Next, cut 1 × 10 gable boards 10 feet long so they'll run "wild" on top (they'll be cut to length after the rafters are up). Cover the gable siding seams with battens, also letting them run wild on top.

4 Frame the Roof

Temporarily attach to the gable siding the ridge board you laid out earlier. It should be 32 inches in from the front of the shed and 26 inches up from the top plate. Then cut pairs of short and long rafters as shown in the rafter detail opposite.

Hold a pair of rafters up against the ridge board gable siding, and mark the outline on the siding; cut to the marked line with a circular saw or reciprocating saw. Repeat at the opposite end. Attach the end rafters to the ridge board, top plate, and siding.

Nail the remaining rafters to the ridge board and secure the opposite end to the top plates with rafter ties. Connect the rafters with 55-inch-long 2 × 4 collar ties.

5 Apply Sheathing and Roofing

For sheathing, use 1 × 10 boards or ¾-inch CDX plywood, starting at the bottom and working up toward the ridge. Add drip edge and 15-pound roofing felt. Install asphalt shingles and ridge caps. (See pages 113 and 115 for more on roofing.)

6 Install the Door and Windows

Using 1 × 10 ship lath boards, 1 × 10s, and 1 × 3s, build a door (see door detail above) to fit the opening. Attach the door to the frame with strap hinges, and add the door latch. If desired, attach screening between the ends of the rafters and the top plates to keep out insects.

Mark window locations in the siding, and cut out the openings with a reciprocating saw or saber saw. Attach each flanged window with galvanized nails, and trim it with 1 × 3 cedar. (See pages 106–109 for more on door and window installation techniques.) Then cut and attach 1 × 6 fascia to the ends of the rafters. Cut and attach corner trim and door trim.

1 × 10 SHIP LAP

HORIZONTAL 1 × 10

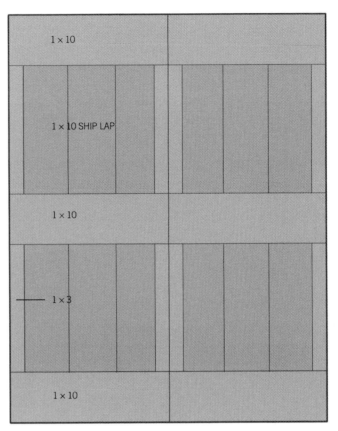

1 × 10

1 × 10 SHIP LAP

1 × 10

1 × 3

1 × 10

DOOR DETAIL

greenhouse shed

Is it a greenhouse? Storage shed? Art studio? Workshop? The answer is yes and then some when you opt for this versatile, light-filled structure. The clear plastic windows of the greenhouse annex, plus the functional double Dutch door and rear window, ensure ample air and light for any use.

Designed in saltbox fashion, this shed gives you the option of orienting the largest portion of the roof to the south for maximum light and heat. However, if you plan to use the shed as an art studio or workshop, orienting the shed northward will provide plenty of indirect light. (To purchase this shed in kit form, see page 160.)
DESIGN: CEDARSHED INDUSTRIES, INC.

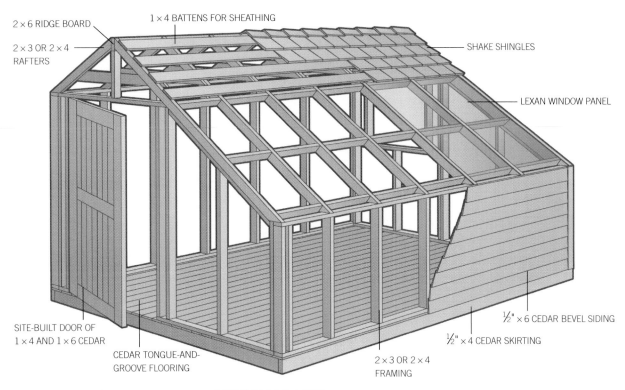

2 × 6 RIDGE BOARD

2 × 3 OR 2 × 4 RAFTERS

1 × 4 BATTENS FOR SHEATHING

SHAKE SHINGLES

LEXAN WINDOW PANEL

SITE-BUILT DOOR OF 1 × 4 AND 1 × 6 CEDAR

CEDAR TONGUE-AND-GROOVE FLOORING

2 × 3 OR 2 × 4 FRAMING

½" × 4 CEDAR SKIRTING

½" × 6 CEDAR BEVEL SIDING

DESIGN DETAILS

Although this stick-framed shed design calls for 2 × 3 framing components, you may want to use conventional 2 × 4s. If you do, be sure to compensate for the added width as you build.

The greenhouse windows are sheets of ¼-inch Lexan. The seams are sealed with self-adhesive foam tape and covered with strips of Lexan that are screwed to the roof frame (page 57). A rear window and front door allow for air circulation.

Simple plant benches can be made to sit under the window by building 32-inch-square frames from 2 × 4s and covering these with hollow-core doors. A layer of plastic laminate bonded to the door face will provide an easy-to-clean surface that's impervious to water (see also the craft table on page 123).

MATERIALS LIST

NAME	DIMENSIONS
Pea gravel and precast concrete piers or concrete for footings	
Floor joists	2 × 6
Tongue-and-groove plywood flooring or	¾"
Cedar tongue-and-groove flooring	1 × 4
Top/bottom plates and wall studs	2 × 3 or 2 × 4
Double top plates	1 × 3 or 1 × 4
Ceiling joists, rafters, and blocking	2 × 3 or 2 × 4
Ridge board	2 × 6
Open sheathing	1 × 4
Cedar roofing shingles and ridge caps	
Cedar bevel siding	½" × 6
Cedar top, skirting, and soffits	½" × 4
Cedar corner trim and bottom skirting	1 × 4
Fascia	1 × 4
Cedar trim	1 × 2
Door	1 × 6, 1 × 4
Lexan window panels, cover strips, foam tape	
Neoprene washers	
4-light window	2' 0" × 2' 4"
Galvanized nails and outdoor screws	
Metal post anchors	
Metal framing brackets and fasteners	
Door hinges and door set	
Paint, stain, or wood preservative	

HOW TO BUILD A GREENHOUSE SHED

The ideal site for a greenhouse is well drained and nearly level, with full exposure to sunlight. The optimum location is on the south or southeast side of your house in a sunny location. The east side is the second best location, since it will capture the most winter sunlight. The next best locations are the southwest and west, with the north side being the least desirable location.

1 Frame the Floor

The floor framing rests on concrete piers or poured footings spaced approximately every 4 feet. To build the frame, lay out joists on two 12-foot rim joists 16 inches on center. Then cut 12 floor joists 93 inches long and attach them to the rim joists with nails or joist hangers. Position the frame on the piers or footings, and level it with shims. Cover the framing with tongue-and-groove pine or cedar flooring or ¾-inch plywood flooring.

2 Build the Walls

Cut four top and bottom plates 12 feet long for the high and low side walls. Then cut seven short wall studs at 37¼ inches and seven long studs at 71¾ inches. Lay out wall studs (pages 101 and 104) at 24 inches on center and build the two side walls. Now lay out the bottom and top plates for the front and back walls (bottom plates are 89 inches, top plates are 46½ inches). The studs are 73⅛ inches, 56⁹⁄₁₆ inches, and 39³⁄₁₆ inches long, going from the tall to the short end; the shorter studs are angled at 36½ degrees on top to match the pitch of the roof. Frame the rough opening for the door (36 inches × 72 inches) and window (26 inches × 30 inches).

3 Raise and Fasten the Walls

Position the rear wall flush with the floor, and screw it to the flooring; brace as needed. Repeat this for the side walls and front wall. Check for level and plumb, and screw the wall sections together at the corners. Before you attach the 2 × 3 or 2 × 4 top plates, lay out rafter locations 24 inches on center.

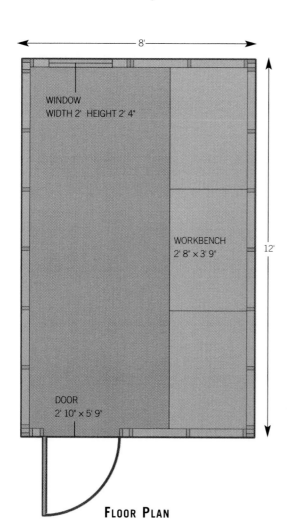

WINDOW
WIDTH 2' HEIGHT 2' 4"

WORKBENCH
2' 8" × 3' 9"

DOOR
2' 10" × 5' 9"

8'

12'

FLOOR PLAN

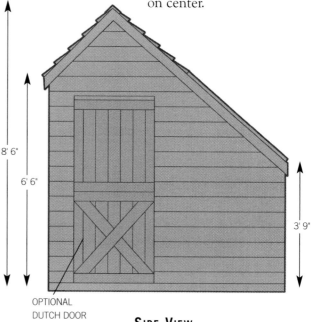

8' 6"

6' 6"

3' 9"

OPTIONAL
DUTCH DOOR

SIDE VIEW

4 Frame the Roof

To frame the roof, start by cutting the rafters to length: The short rafters are 28¹³⁄₁₆ inches long and the long rafters are 86¹³⁄₁₆ inches long. Both the short and long rafters are mitered at the peak at 36½ degrees. Attach the end rafters to a 12-foot-long ridge board and place this on the wall frame. Attach the free ends of the rafters to the walls by screwing up through the top plates and into the rafters. Install the remaining rafters 24 inches on center along the ridge board. Cut and install sets of blocking between the rafters centered 59 inches and 29 inches up from the outside edge of the short wall. Cut and install collar ties and attach them to the rafters (see framing detail).

5 Install the Greenhouse Windows

Cut four pieces of ¼-inch Lexan 23¼ inches wide by 60 inches long, and two pieces 24¾ inches by 60 inches long (these are placed adjacent to the fascia ends of the roof). Apply double-sided foam tape the length of the rafters and remove the plastic protective film from the Lexan and place the panels on the roof frame. Apply foam tape over the seams and cover these with 1½-inch-wide, 60-inch-long Lexan strips. Drill ⅛-inch holes through the strip and panel and into the rafters every 12 inches. Secure with 2-inch screws and neoprene washers. Install the rear window and build a door to fit the opening and mount it with door hinges. Install handle hardware or door lockset.

6 Shingle the Roof

To cover the ridge portion of the roof frame with cedar shingles, start by cutting and attaching 1 × 4 open sheathing on both sides of the ridge. Install the remaining open sheathing, spacing them apart for the desired shingle exposure. Attach shingles to 1 × 4 battens, working from the bottom up. Install cap shingles along the ridge. (See pages 113 and 115 for other roofing materials and techniques.)

7 Enclose the Walls

Apply ½-inch × 6-inch bevel siding, starting at the bottom and working up, using a 1-inch overlap and 6d galvanized nails. Cut and install window trim, door trim, and shutter trim as desired. Final trim includes corner trim, 1 × 4 fascia on the ends of rafters, and ½-inch × 4-inch soffits, along with top and bottom skirting. (See pages 102 and 105 for more on siding materials and techniques.)

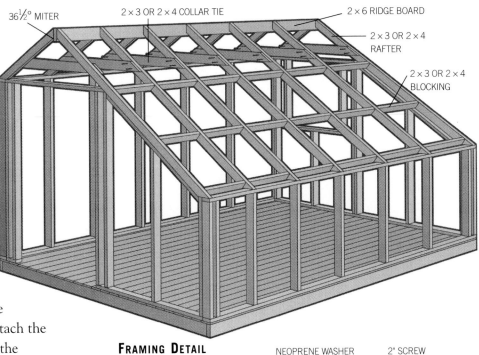

36½° MITER   2 × 3 OR 2 × 4 COLLAR TIE   2 × 6 RIDGE BOARD   2 × 3 OR 2 × 4 RAFTER   2 × 3 OR 2 × 4 BLOCKING

FRAMING DETAIL

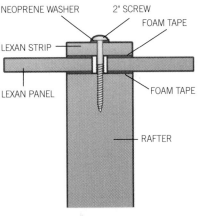

NEOPRENE WASHER   2" SCREW   FOAM TAPE   LEXAN STRIP   LEXAN PANEL   FOAM TAPE   RAFTER

PANEL DETAIL

lean-to shed

When you just want covered space, plain and simple, look to the lean-to. The design is pure function: The shed leans against an existing structure to protect firewood, outdoor furniture, garden tools, or toys against the elements. Build this in a day and put it to work right away.

While most lean-to sheds live up to their name by "leaning" into another structure, they can also be freestanding. And if it suits your purposes, you can locate the door in the tall wall—ideal if you are wheeling in lawn or garden equipment. (To purchase plans for this shed, see page 160.)

DESIGN: GARLINGHOUSE COMPANY.

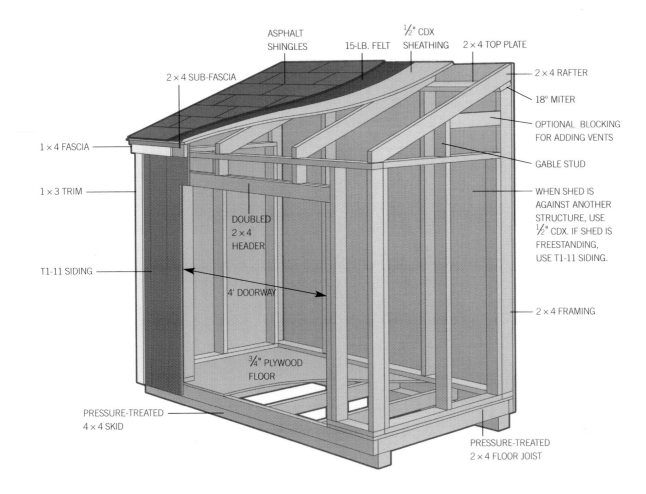

Labels on diagram:
- ASPHALT SHINGLES
- 15-LB. FELT
- ½" CDX SHEATHING
- 2 × 4 TOP PLATE
- 2 × 4 SUB-FASCIA
- 2 × 4 RAFTER
- 18° MITER
- OPTIONAL BLOCKING FOR ADDING VENTS
- GABLE STUD
- 1 × 4 FASCIA
- 1 × 3 TRIM
- WHEN SHED IS AGAINST ANOTHER STRUCTURE, USE ½" CDX. IF SHED IS FREESTANDING, USE T1-11 SIDING.
- DOUBLED 2 × 4 HEADER
- T1-11 SIDING
- 4' DOORWAY
- 2 × 4 FRAMING
- ¾" PLYWOOD FLOOR
- PRESSURE-TREATED 4 × 4 SKID
- PRESSURE-TREATED 2 × 4 FLOOR JOIST

DESIGN DETAILS

The slanting roof is designed to shed water in only one direction; this means that the back wall is mostly unprotected where the shed attaches to another structure. Because of this, the rear wall is sheathed with ½-inch CDX. If you plan to make this a freestanding shed, consider using concrete piers or poured footings and make sure to sheath the back wall with exterior-rated T1-11 siding like the rest of the walls.

Like many sheds, this type can adjust in size to suit your needs. The shed shown above is 8 feet long; the shed pictured opposite is 6 feet long, having one less 24-inch on-center stud and rafter.

MATERIALS LIST

NAME	DIMENSIONS
Pressure-treated skids	4 × 4
Pressure-treated floor joists	2 × 4
Tongue-and-groove plywood flooring	¾"
Bottom plates, studs, header, rafters, top plate gable studs, cripple studs, nailer, door framing, and sub-fascia	2 × 4
Top plate	1 × 4
T1-11 wall sheathing (use cutout for door)	
CDX rear wall and roof sheathing	½"
Door trim	1 × 3
Fascia and rake trim	1 × 4
Drip edge and 15-lb. roofing felt	
Asphalt shingles	
Galvanized nails and outdoor screws	
Metal framing brackets and fasteners	
Door hinges and latch	
Paint, stain, or wood preservative	

HOW TO BUILD A LEAN-TO SHED

The lean-to shed shown here is 4 feet deep by 6 feet wide, but it's easy to expand to 8 feet in width by adding another stud to the back wall and increasing the spacing of the door studs to 24 inches from the ends. The floor frame and roofing also would have to be expanded. You might also want to add vents to the gable ends near the high point of the back wall under the fascia.

1 Frame the Floor

The floor frame of this relatively small shed rests on skids instead of a foundation; cut two pressure-treated 4 × 4s to a length of 6 feet. Do the same with two 2 × 4 pressure-treated rim joists. Lay out floor joists on the rim joists (see page 101 and 104) 16 inches on center. Cut six floor joists to a length of 45 inches, and position them between the rim joists; secure with 16d nails. Place the frame on the skids, square it up, and toenail the floor joists to the skids. Cover the frame with ¾-inch tongue and groove plywood.

2 Build the Walls

Starting with the rear, build the walls in sections. Cut 6-foot-long top and bottom plates and lay out studs 24 inches on center. The wall studs are 8 feet long, with the top ends mitered at 18 degrees. Build the rear wall and attach it the floor frame, bracing as necessary (see page 28). The top plate for the front wall is 6 feet long; the two bottom plates are 1 foot long. Mark the door opening (4 feet wide) and the stud positions. Cut four wall studs 81¼ inches long and install. Cut two 51-inch-long 2 × 4s for a header and nail together. Install 73-inch-long jack studs and attach the header. Cut and attach 6¼-inch-long cripple studs. Attach the front wall to the floor and brace as needed. The side walls use 41-inch-long top and bottom plates; studs are 81¼ inches. Build the side walls and attach to the floor. When wall sections are square and plumb, screw the corners together.

3 Frame the Roof

The roof framing consists of 2 × 4 rafters that rest on the top plates of the rear and front walls. Cut four rafters to size (see rafter detail). Toenail these to the top and bottom plates every 24 inches. Cut two gable studs to fit between the end rafters and the top plate of the side wall. Cut the 2 × 4 sub-fascia to length and attach to the front ends of the rafters. Cut and install the fascia.

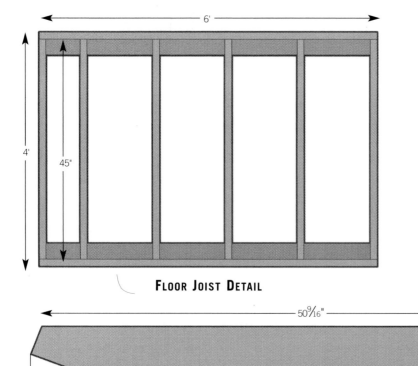

FLOOR JOIST DETAIL

50⁹/₁₆"

3⁵/₁₆"   46⁷/₈"   72°

RAFTER DETAIL

4 Enclose the Walls

Cut pieces of T1-11 to cover the front and the sides. Position the siding flush with the bottom of the rim joists, and attach it with 8d galvanized nails every 8 inches or so. Cut ½-inch CDX plywood to cover the rear wall; make sure it extends up to cover the rafters.

5 Sheath the Rafters

Use ½-inch CDX plywood to sheath the rafters. Stagger the plywood joints so they don't end up on the same rafter. Before nailing in place with 6d nails, verify that the rafters are 24 inches on center. Cut the rake trim to cover the exposed edges of the roof sheathing, and attach. Install drip edge, add 15-pound roofing felt, and apply the shingles. (For more on roofing materials and techniques, see pages 113 and 115.)

6 Build a Door

Using the T1-11 cutout left over from cutting the door opening, build a door, trimming it out with 1 × 3 (see door detail). Attach the doors with strap hinges and add a door latch. Cut and install corner and perimeter door trim.

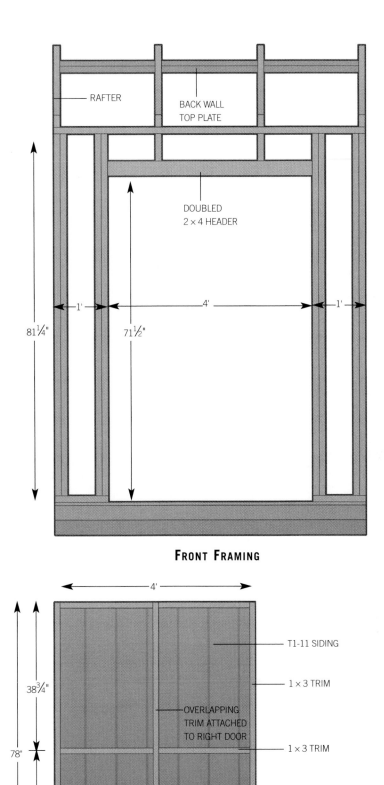

RAFTER

BACK WALL TOP PLATE

DOUBLED 2 × 4 HEADER

81¼"

71½"

1'   4'   1'

FRONT FRAMING

4'

T1-11 SIDING

1 × 3 TRIM

OVERLAPPING TRIM ATTACHED TO RIGHT DOOR

1 × 3 TRIM

38¾"

78"

38¼"

LEFT DOOR

RIGHT DOOR

1' 10¾"   2' 1¼"

DOOR DETAIL

five-sided cabana

Make smart use of any corner space with this distinctive, five-sided shed that nestles right into a landscape. French doors let in air and light (you might opt for Dutch doors for a more informal look), while windows help illuminate the 56 square feet.

If you have some carpentry experience and are looking for an attractive, challenging shed project, this is the one. You'll want to rent or buy a compound miter saw to cut the hip-roof rafters and make a neat job of the trim and siding. (To purchase this shed in kit form, see Resources, page 160.)

DESIGN: SUMMERWOOD PRODUCTS.

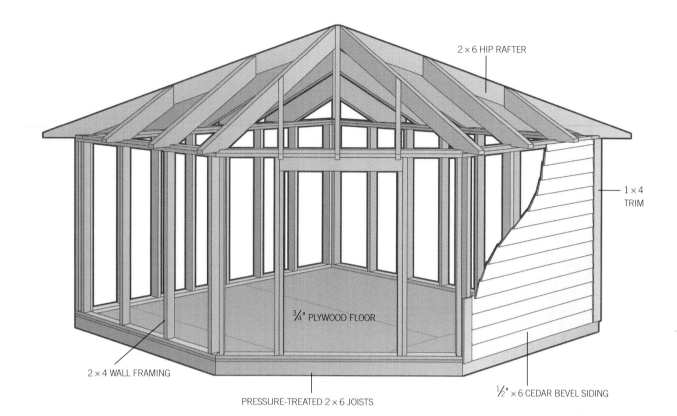

2 × 6 HIP RAFTER

1 × 4 TRIM

¾" PLYWOOD FLOOR

2 × 4 WALL FRAMING

PRESSURE-TREATED 2 × 6 JOISTS

½" × 6 CEDAR BEVEL SIDING

DESIGN DETAILS

The advantage of a five-sided design is that it's perfect for slipping into a corner. The disadvantage is that the roof framing is very complex; this portion of the project is best tackled by experienced DIY-ers or a professional framer. Fortunately, the floor and wall framing are fairly straightforward.

If you plan to use the shed as a potting shed or workshop, consider adding side windows (shown opposite). The door framing can be altered to suit a single, instead of a double, door (see pages 39 and 41 for framing details).

MATERIALS LIST

NAME	DIMENSIONS
Pea gravel and precast concrete piers or concrete for footings	
Pressure-treated rim/floor joists	2 × 6
Top/bottom plates, wall studs	2 × 4
Door header, window spacer	2 × 4
Tongue-and-groove plywood flooring	¾"
Hip, front, and rear rafters	2 × 6
Jack and center rafters	2 × 4
Double top plates	2 × 4
6-light flanged window (optional)	2' 0" × 2' 4"
Doors (unless site-built)	18" × 6' 8"
CDX roof sheathing	⅝"
Drip edge and 15-lb. roofing felt	
Asphalt shingles and ridge caps	
Cedar bevel siding	½" × 6"
Cedar soffits, fascia, corner trim, skirting, door casing, threshold	1 × 6
Galvanized nails and outdoor screws	
Metal post anchors	
Metal framing brackets and fasteners	
Strap hinges and door latch	
Paint, stain, or wood preservative	

HOW TO BUILD A FIVE-SIDED CABANA

If you're planning on using skids for a foundation, use 4 × 6 pressure-treated beams—one centered, and the other two 36 inches to each side. Concrete piers or poured footings should be set in 2 inches along the front and back edges of the shed and spaced roughly 5 feet apart; another set should be centered on the width of the shed. Span the skids, piers, or footings with pressure-treated 2 × 6s and attach them with anchor bolts. Alternatively, install a slab foundation; make sure to have the contractor install anchor bolts around the perimeter.

Roof framing for this five-sided shed is complex and is best done on the sheathed floor frame before the walls are erected. Then it can be lifted onto the walls once they're in place.

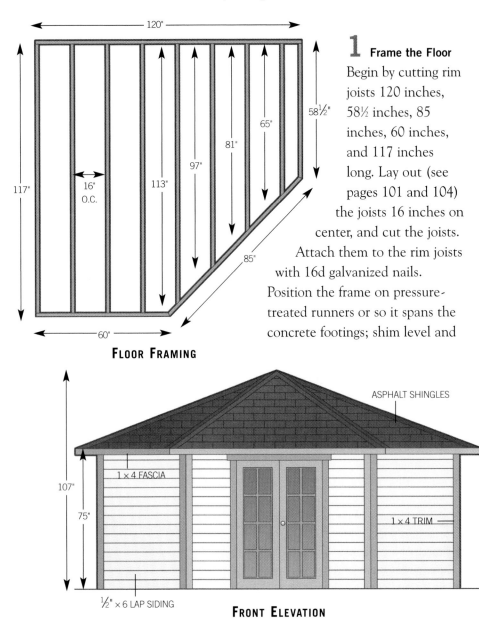

FLOOR FRAMING

1 Frame the Floor

Begin by cutting rim joists 120 inches, 58½ inches, 85 inches, 60 inches, and 117 inches long. Lay out (see pages 101 and 104) the joists 16 inches on center, and cut the joists. Attach them to the rim joists with 16d galvanized nails. Position the frame on pressure-treated runners or so it spans the concrete footings; shim level and toenail the frame to the runners. Cover the frame with plywood tongue and groove flooring, fastening it with 8d galvanized nails.

2 Frame the Hip Roof

While hip roofs can be framed after the walls are raised, you'll find it easier to fit and refit the compound miters of rafters if you frame the roof on the floor, raising it in place later. That way you can attack some very complex framing at a convenient working level.

The roof slope is 4 in 12 on the sides and back, and 10 in 12 on the front. Start by cutting a set of double top plates, temporarily attaching them around the perimeter of the floor frame with screws. Attach the ends of the plates together with 3½-inch deck screws. Mark the center of each back wall and the front wall.

Cut the two 2 × 6 hip rafters that run from the left corner to the right corner. Cut the top ends at a 4 in 12 slope. Angle-cut the bottom ends of the rafters to fit over the top plates with a 12-inch overhang. When you are satisfied with the angle cuts, fasten the hip rafters together and temporarily screw them to the top plates. Next, cut and install the front and rear 2 × 4 rafters. After adding 2 × 4 common rafters, install the jack rafters 16 inches on center.

ASPHALT SHINGLES

1 × 4 FASCIA

1 × 4 TRIM

½" × 6 LAP SIDING

FRONT ELEVATION

3 Build Wall Sections

Remove the screws holding the framed roof to the floor and set it aside. Cut bottom plates to match the top plates. Then lay out the wall studs and rough openings. Cut enough wall studs 72 inches long for 16-inch-on-center spacing, and assemble each wall. Frame rough openings by adding jack studs, headers, cripple studs, and sills as required (the door opening is 36½ inches wide and the full height of the wall).

Note that the top and bottom plates for the right and left walls are mitered at 22½ degrees on the ends that connect to the front wall. (For more on framing, see pages 26–29 and 107.)

4 Raise the Walls

Set the right rear wall on the floor and secure it by driving screws through the bottom plate into the floor frame. Brace the wall temporarily (see page 28) and then raise the left rear wall, followed by the side walls and the front wall. Check for plumb and secure the walls to each other at the corners.

5 Add Roof Sheathing

Before attaching the framed roof to the shed, it's easiest now to precut ⅜-inch sheathing to cover the frame. Label all pieces and set them aside. With helpers, lift the framed roof onto the shed walls. Secure it to the walls by screwing down through the double top plates into the top plates of the

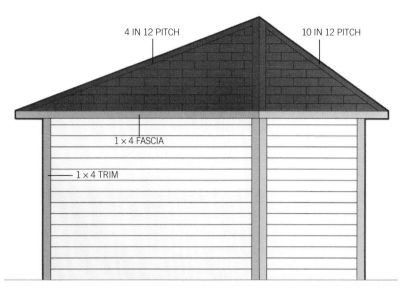

SIDE VIEW

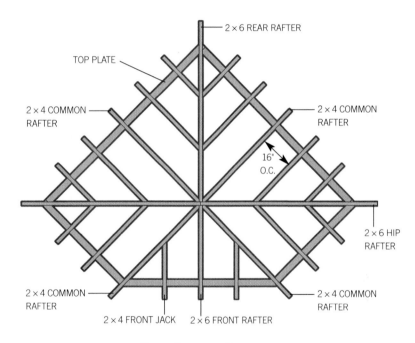

ROOF FRAMING DETAIL

walls. Add the sheathing, drip edge, roofing felt, and shingles.

6 Install the Windows and Doors

Install windows in rough openings. Install prehung doors, or build a board-and-batten door to fit the rough opening and attach it with strap hinges and a latch.

7 Add Siding and Trim

To enclose the walls, cut and install siding horizontally, starting from the bottom and working to the top plate. Allow the bottom edge of the first piece to overhang the bottom plate by ¾ inch. Cut and install the soffits, fascia, and corner trim. Trim around the windows; add shutter trim if desired.

hip-roof shed

Whether this hip-roof shed houses garden tools or a poolside changing room, its lines lend a little formality to dress up the structure's functionality. Since the roof overhang surrounds the structure, eaves offer unbroken protection. The distinctive roof line is a construction challenge.

Mock shutters and some variation on the trim give this shed an understated style. Coupled with horizontal ship-lap siding and multipaned door and windows, this shed would be an asset to any property. (To purchase this shed in kit form, see Resources, page 160.)

Design: Summerwood Products.

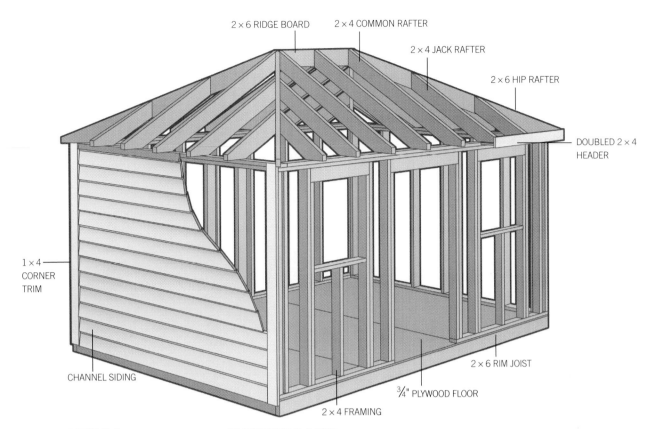

2 × 6 RIDGE BOARD 2 × 4 COMMON RAFTER

2 × 4 JACK RAFTER

2 × 6 HIP RAFTER

DOUBLED 2 × 4 HEADER

1 × 4 CORNER TRIM

CHANNEL SIDING

2 × 4 FRAMING

¾" PLYWOOD FLOOR

2 × 6 RIM JOIST

DESIGN DETAILS

The simple floor and wall framing on this shed is adaptable to suit your requirements. The 8-foot by 12-foot version illustrated above can easily be revised to suit a smaller footprint. The framing for the hip roof, on the other hand, is complex and can be frustrating for a first-time builder. (For more on hip roofs, see page 112.) The easiest way to do it is to build the roof frame on the shed floor before erecting the walls. Then, with the aid of some strong helpers, the framed roof can be lifted onto the completed walls.

If you're not comfortable framing the roof, consider hiring out just that portion of the job. Once the roof is framed and installed, the sheathing and roofing are easy to install.

MATERIALS LIST

NAME	DIMENSIONS
Pea gravel and precast concrete piers or concrete for footings	
Optional pressure-treated runners	2 × 6
Pressure-treated rim/floor joists	2 × 6
Top/bottom plates, wall studs, door header, window spacer, common and jack rafters	2 × 4
Tongue-and-groove plywood flooring	¾"
Ridge board and hip rafters	2 × 6
4-light flanged windows (optional)	2' 0" × 2' 4"
Door	3' 0" × 6' 8"
CDX roof sheathing	⅝"
Drip edge, 15-lb. roofing felt	
Asphalt shingles and ridge caps	
Channel cedar siding	¾" × 6
Cedar soffits, fascia, corner trim, door and door casing, and threshold	1 × 4
Galvanized nails	
Outdoor screws	
Metal post anchors	
Metal framing brackets and fasteners	
Strap hinges and door latch	
Paint, stain, or wood preservative	

HOW TO BUILD A HIP-ROOF SHED

If you plan to use skids for a foundation, use three 12-foot-long 4 × 6 pressure-treated beams; one centered and the other two 42 inches to each side. Concrete piers or poured footings should be set 6 inches in along the width of the shed and spaced 36 inches apart, and set in 16 inches along the length of the shed and spaced 56 inches apart. (For foundation options, see pages 98–99.) Span the piers or footings with 12-foot pressure-treated 2 × 6s, and attach them with anchor bolts.

1 Frame the Floor

Build the floor frame by first cutting rim joists 144 inches long. Lay out the joists 16 inches on center (see page 101) and cut joists 93 inches long. Attach these to the rim joists with 16d nails or joist hangers. Position the frame on the runners and shim level; check the diagonals, and when square, toenail the frame to the runners. Cover the frame with tongue and groove plywood.

2 Frame the Roof

The simplest way to frame the roof is to build it on the floor frame before the walls are erected and then place it on the shed when complete. The roof pitch is 7 in 12. To start, cut a set of double top plates and temporarily attach them around the perimeter of the floor frame with screws; attach the ends of the plates together with 3½-inch deck screws.

Mark the center of each side frame and the center of the ridge board. Cut the six common rafters

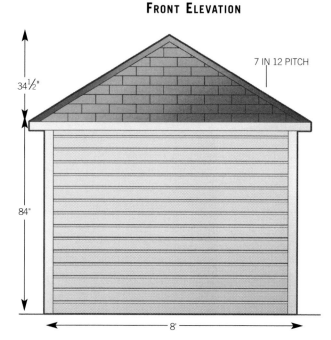

FRONT ELEVATION

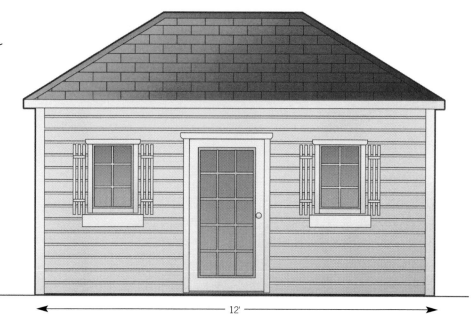

SIDE ELEVATION

for the sides and notch the ends to fit over the top plates. Secure one end of the rafters to the ridge board and the other end to the top plates. Attach two shorter common rafters to the ends of the ridge board and to the top plates. Cut and install the four hip rafters angled from the corner of the wall to the ridge board. Cut and attach the 16 jack rafters; ends connecting to the hip rafters will have to be mitered to match the hip rafter angle. Remove the screws holding the framed roof in place and set it aside.

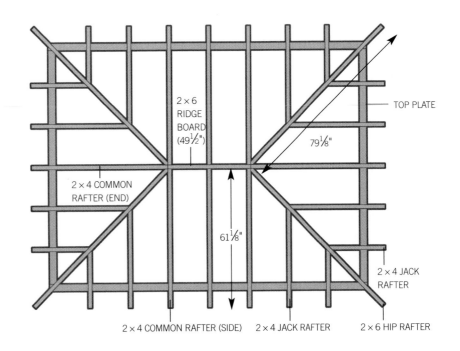

ROOF FRAMING DETAIL

3 Frame the Walls

To build each wall section, first cut matching top and bottom plates to length. Then lay out the wall studs and rough openings. Cut enough wall studs 72 inches long for 16-inch-on-center spacing, and assemble each wall. Frame rough openings by adding jack studs, headers, cripple studs, and sills as required.

4 Raise and Secure the Walls

Set the first wall on the floor, and secure the wall by driving screws through the bottom plate into the floor frame. Brace the wall temporarily (see page 28), and raise and secure the remaining wall sections in the same way. Check for plumb, and secure the walls to each other at the corners.

5 Add the Roof Sheathing

Before attaching the framed roof to the shed, it's easiest now to precut ⅝-inch sheathing to cover the frame. Label all pieces and set them aside. With the help of four strong helpers, lift the framed roof onto the shed walls. Secure the roof frame to the walls by screwing down through the double top plates into the top plates of the walls. Add the sheathing, drip edge, roofing felt, shingles, and ridge caps. (For roofing options, see pages 113 and 115.)

6 Apply Siding and Trim

To enclose the walls, cut and install cedar channel siding horizontally, starting from the bottom and working to the top plate.

(Note: If you're using flanged windows, install them before the siding.) Allow the bottom edge of the first piece to overhang the bottom plate by ¾ inch. Cut and install the soffits, fascia, and corner trim.

7 Install the Door

Install a prehung door or build a board-and-batten door to fit the rough opening, and attach it with strap hinges and a door latch. Trim around the door and windows, and add the shutter trim if desired.

two-car reverse gable garage

While the garage accommodates vehicles, the extra work or storage space on the second floor of this model is an added bonus. Light pours in from the side windows and dormer to brighten the 24- by 26-foot space of this versatile, two-story design.

Far from the usual cookie-cutter two-car garage, this structure was designed to complement a turn-of-the-century home. It illustrates the advantage of building upward to add usable space to a garage without crowding the lot.

DESIGN: W. ALEX TEIPEL, ARCHITECTURAL RESOURCES.

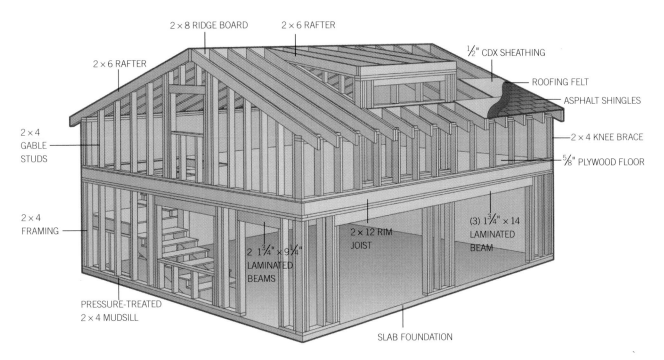

2 × 8 RIDGE BOARD

2 × 6 RAFTER

½" CDX SHEATHING

ROOFING FELT

ASPHALT SHINGLES

2 × 6 RAFTER

2 × 4 KNEE BRACE

⅝" PLYWOOD FLOOR

2 × 4 GABLE STUDS

2 × 4 FRAMING

(3) 1¾" × 14 LAMINATED BEAM

2 × 12 RIM JOIST

2 1¾" × 9¼" LAMINATED BEAMS

PRESSURE-TREATED 2 × 4 MUDSILL

SLAB FOUNDATION

DESIGN DETAILS

This two-story reverse gable garage rests on a slab foundation. Stairs inside lead to the second floor, which can be used for storage or as a workspace. An optional dormer provides added headroom and pulls in natural light.

The roof pitch is 6 in 12 for the standard rafters and 4 in 12 for the dormer. If the additional space isn't needed, you can build this without the second floor— just reduce the joists to 2 × 8s and leave out the second floor knee walls.

The beam supporting the second-story joists can be eliminated by running 14-inch I-joists (a composite wood material) from the front plates to the back.

MATERIALS LIST

NAME	DIMENSIONS
Crushed stone, rebar, welded wire mesh, and concrete for T-shaped slab foundation	
Pressure-treated mudsill	2 × 4
Plates and wall studs	2 × 4
Rafters and collar ties	2 × 6
Trim, headers, ridge board, and rafters	2 × 8
Floor joists and trim	2 × 12
Laminated veneer lumber headers	1¾" × 14"
Laminated veneer lumber headers	1¾" × 9¼"
Laminated veneer lumber central beam	1¾" × 18"
Pipe support column	3½"-diameter
Tongue-and-groove plywood flooring	⅝"
CDX wall and roof sheathing	½"
Drip edge and 15-lb. roofing felt	
Asphalt shingles and ridge caps	
Beveled siding	½" x 6
Vapor retarder	
Overhead doors	8' 0" × 9' 0'''
Prehung door, door set	3' 0" × 6' 8"
Dormer windows	1' 8" × 1' 3"
Gable windows	2' 0" × 3' 0"
Side windows	2' 4" × 4' 0"
Fascia	1 × 8, 1 × 10
Corner trim	⁵⁄₄" × 4"
Galvanized nails and outdoor screws, metal post anchors, framing brackets, and fasteners	
Paint, stain, or wood preservative	

HOW TO BUILD A TWO-CAR REVERSE GABLE GARAGE

Laminated veneer lumber (LVL) or "glu-lams" can be ordered at most full-service lumberyards. These engineered beams are formed by layering thin wood veneers with waterproof adhesive and compressing them in a heated press. LVL is available in various thicknesses and widths and is easy to work using conventional tools.

1 Pour the Foundation

Excavate for the T-shaped foundation, install #4 rebar around the perimeter trench, and build forms. Add a layer of pea gravel or crushed stone and pour concrete for the footings. When the footings have cured, pour the concrete for the slab and the footings for the support posts (see section drawing, opposite). Level and smooth the concrete, and install the anchor bolts in the still-wet concrete. Cover with the slab with plastic and keep it damp for two to three days.

2 Frame the Floor

Cut pressure-treated 2 × 4 mudsills for the perimeter. Transfer the anchor bolt locations, and drill holes in the mudsills. Cut top plates to match the mudsills, and lay out wall studs 16 inches on center (see page 104) on pairs of mudsills/top plates. Lay out the rough openings for the first-floor windows, the entrance door, and the overhead doors. Cut sufficient studs to length (96 inches), and build the walls in sections. Add the jack studs, LVL headers, cripple studs, and sills.

3 Raise the Walls

Beginning with the gable ends, place the wall section over the anchor bolts, slip on washers, and thread on nuts; tighten them only friction-tight. Temporarily brace each wall (see page 28), and continue until all four walls are up. Check for square, level, and plumb, and then screw the walls together at the corners and fully tighten the nuts on the mudsills.

4 Install the Beam

Cut and install the LVL beam that spans the eaves walls. This beam is 13 feet 8 inches in from the gable wall with the entry door, and it rests on the steel pipe column. The 2 × 12 second-floor joists rest on this beam near the center of the garage. Cut rim joists for the second-floor joists, and lay out floor joists 16 inches on center, doubling up every other joist. Then cut floor joists to length for both sides and attach them to the rim joists with

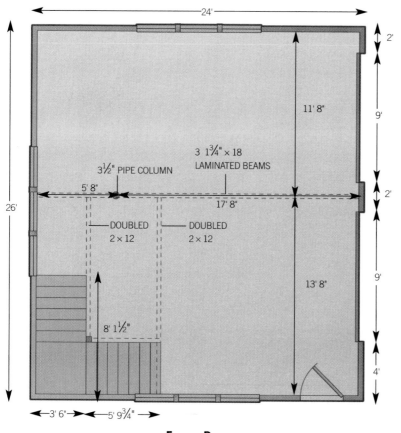

FLOOR PLAN

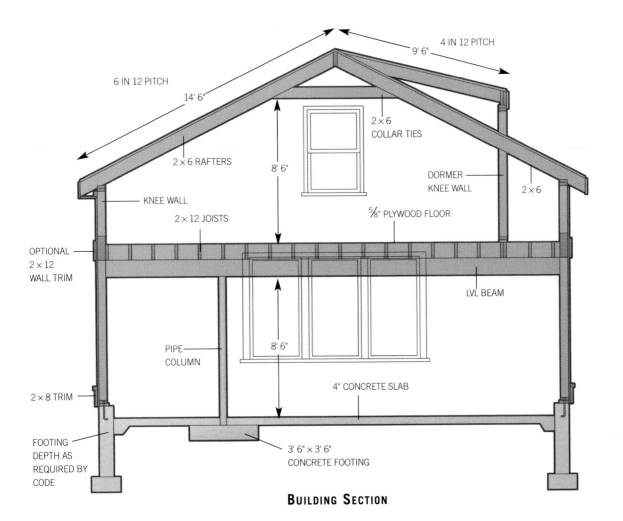

4 IN 12 PITCH

9' 6"

6 IN 12 PITCH

14' 6"

2 × 6 COLLAR TIES

2 × 6 RAFTERS

8' 6"

DORMER KNEE WALL

2 × 6

KNEE WALL

2 × 12 JOISTS

⅝" PLYWOOD FLOOR

OPTIONAL 2 × 12 WALL TRIM

LVL BEAM

PIPE COLUMN

8' 6"

4" CONCRETE SLAB

2 × 8 TRIM

3' 6" × 3' 6" CONCRETE FOOTING

FOOTING DEPTH AS REQUIRED BY CODE

BUILDING SECTION

joist hangers. Attach the other end to the LVL beam with hurricane ties. Cover the joists with ⅝-inch tongue-and-groove plywood.

5 Frame the Second Floor

On the second floor, measure and cut top and bottom plates for the eaves and gable knee walls; lay out studs 16 inches on center. Cut knee wall studs to length (25¾ inches) and install between the top plates. Attach the knee walls to the second-floor frame. Cut double top plates, mark rafter locations on the eaves plates, and install. Note that the dormer knee wall is 3 feet, 8 inches higher than the front eaves knee wall; also,

the rafters are shorter and cut for a 4 in 12 pitch versus a 6 in 12 pitch for the regular rafters.

6 Frame the Roof

Start framing the roof by cutting a 2 × 8 ridge board to length. Make a rafter template and cut rafters to length; the gable is 14 feet, 6 inches; the dormer, 9 foot 6 inches. (See page 114 for how to cut rafters.) Attach pairs of rafters to the ends of the ridge board and lift them onto the knee walls; attach with rafter ties. Install the remaining rafters, then cut and install the gable wall studs to fit between the rafters and the gable knee walls. Cut

and install collar ties (9 feet 3 inches). Note that the loose ends of the dormer studs rest on top of the dormer knee wall. Sheath the roof frame with ½-inch CDX; add drip edge, 15-pound roofing felt, asphalt shingles, and the ridge caps.

7 Sheath and Add Siding

Enclose the garage walls by first installing ½-inch CDX sheathing. Cover this with a vapor retarder and install the windows and doors. Then cut and install 2 × 8 and 2 × 12 trim, 1 × 10 fascia, 1 × 8 gable fascia, and ¾ × 4-inch corner trim. Complete the structure by adding the beveled siding.

two-car hip-roof garage

Get multipurpose use with classic design when you add this structure to your property. The hip roof features complete perimeter overhangs, which protect the structure from weather. Inside, the 24- by 36-foot space fits two cars, with plenty of space for extra storage and living or work space.

The framing for the hip roof is simplified with the use of three types of trusses that combine with a few compound-mitered jack rafters and hip rafters to complete the roof framing. While still a project for a homeowner with framing experience, this approach spares you the challenge of a stick-built hip roof.

DESIGN: GARAGES, ETC.

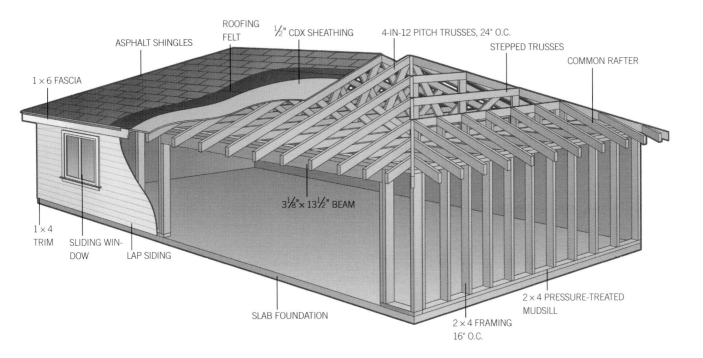

ASPHALT SHINGLES

ROOFING FELT

½" CDX SHEATHING

4-IN-12 PITCH TRUSSES, 24" O.C.

STEPPED TRUSSES

COMMON RAFTER

1 × 6 FASCIA

1 × 4 TRIM

SLIDING WINDOW

LAP SIDING

3⅛" × 13½" BEAM

SLAB FOUNDATION

2 × 4 FRAMING 16" O.C.

2 × 4 PRESSURE-TREATED MUDSILL

DESIGN DETAILS

The stick-framed walls are easy to build and erect. The challenge is the hip roof. The designer used preengineered roof trusses to simplify hip-roof framing, but it can also be stick-framed (see pages 69 and 112). If you're not comfortable framing the roof, consider hiring out that portion of the job. Once the framing is completed, the sheathing and roofing are easy to install.

You could easily modify the design to make this a three-car garage by simply adding a single overhead door in place of the sliding window. If you do this, use a 4 × 12 header and order additional 2 × 6 cedar door wrap.

MATERIALS LIST

NAME	DIMENSIONS
Pea gravel and concrete for slab foundation	
Rebar	#4
Pressure-treated mudsills	2 × 4
Plates and wall/cripple studs	2 × 4
Window header	2 × 4
Beam for overhead door header	3⅛" × 13½"
Cedar door wrap	2 × 6
Cedar fascia	1 × 6
Cedar corner trim and window wrap	1 × 4
Cedar trim	1 × 3
OSB wall sheathing	⁷⁄₁₆"
CDX roof sheathing	½"
Prehung door	3' 0' × 6' 8"
Sliding window	5' 0' × 3' 0'
Preengineered trusses with 4 in 12 slope vapor retarder	
Lap siding	½" × 6
Overhead door	16' × 8'
Galvanized nails and outdoor screws	
Metal post anchors	
Metal framing brackets and fasteners	
Door set	
Paint, stain, or wood preservative	

HOW TO BUILD A TWO-CAR HIP-ROOF GARAGE

As with the three-car reverse gable garage shown on page 82, this hip-roof garage also uses cedar to "wrap" the rough openings of the windows and doors and double as trim. Also, the side entrance door can be installed on either side of the garage (or even the rear wall) and located toward the front on back, whichever suits your plans best.

1 Pour the Slab

Excavate for the slab foundation, install #4 rebar around the perimeter trench, and build forms. Add a layer of pea gravel or crushed stone; pour the concrete. Level and smooth the concrete, locate anchor positions for the mudsills, and install them in the still-wet concrete. Cure by covering the slab with plastic sheets, and keep damp two to three days.

2 Frame the Walls

Cut 2 × 4 pressure-treated mudsills for the perimeter. Transfer anchor locations, and drill holes for the bolts to pass through. Cut top plates to match the mudsills, and lay out wall studs 16 inches on center (see page 101) on pairs of mudsills/top plates. Also lay out rough openings for the window, a side door, and the overhead door. (Note: The overhead door rough opening is 1½ inches higher and 3 inches wider than normal to allow for the addition of 2 × 6 cedar door wrap.) Cut sufficient studs to length (96 inches) and build the walls in sections. Add jack studs, headers, cripple studs, and sills as required.

3 Raise the Walls

Starting with the side walls, place the wall section over the anchor bolts, slip on washers, and thread on nuts; tighten only friction-tight. Brace each wall as necessary and continue until all four walls are up. Check for square, level, and plumb. Then screw the walls together at the corners and fully tighten the nuts on the mudsills. Next, cut double top plates, mark the truss locations every 24 inches

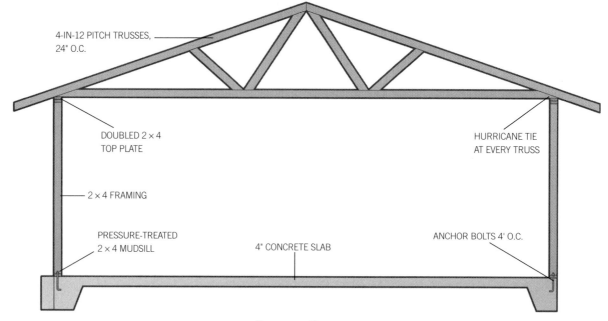

4-IN-12 PITCH TRUSSES, 24" O.C.

DOUBLED 2 × 4 TOP PLATE

HURRICANE TIE AT EVERY TRUSS

2 × 4 FRAMING

PRESSURE-TREATED 2 × 4 MUDSILL

4" CONCRETE SLAB

ANCHOR BOLTS 4' O.C.

BUILDING SECTION

ROOF FRAMING DETAIL

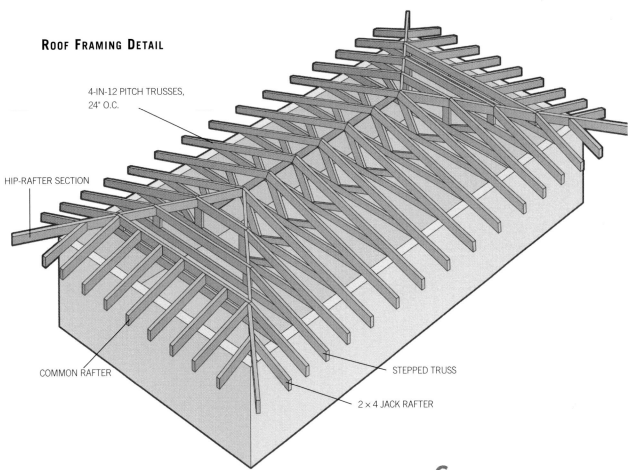

4-IN-12 PITCH TRUSSES, 24" O.C.

HIP-RAFTER SECTION

COMMON RAFTER

STEPPED TRUSS

2 × 4 JACK RAFTER

on center on the eaves plates, and install the double top plates.

4 Frame the Roof

Roof framing is simplified with the use of preengineered trusses (see the roof framing detail, above). There are seven common trusses and three "stepped" trusses on each side of these. Start by attaching the center common truss to the double top plates, using rafter ties. Brace as needed. Then add the remaining trusses 24-inch on center, working toward the ends. Cut and attach hip rafters to the high point of

the end common rafters (the hip rafters rest on *top* of the stepped trusses). Attach the loose ends of the hip rafters to the double top plates with rafter ties. Finally, cut and attach common and jack rafters to fit between the hip rafters and the double top rafters.

5 Apply the Roofing

Cover the roof framing with ½-inch CDX, and add drip edge and 15-pound roofing felt. Cover it with asphalt shingles and install the ridge caps. (For other roofing options, see pages 113 and 115.)

6 Add the Siding

To enclose the walls, start by cutting and installing sheathing. Cover this with a vapor retarder and install the sliding window and prehung door. Then cut and attach 6-inch lap siding.

7 Apply the Trim

Cut and install the 1 × 6 cedar fascia, 1 × 4 cedar corner boards and window wrap, and 1 × 3 cedar window trim. Install the overhead door, or have it installed professionally.

two-car gable with summer room

Space and grace combine in this expansive, 24-foot by 38-foot structure, designed for two cars. The attached summer room boasts windows on three sides, a half bath, and even a fireplace. Because the room's ceiling is open to the rafters, it seems even bigger (and better).

Designed to complement a mid-nineteenth-century home, this structure is elegantly detailed, with features more common on a cottage than on a garage. While truly a project for homeowners with advanced skills, this garage is loaded with ideas that can be adapted to more modest structures.

DESIGN: W. ALEX TEIPEL, ARCHITECTURAL RESOURCES.

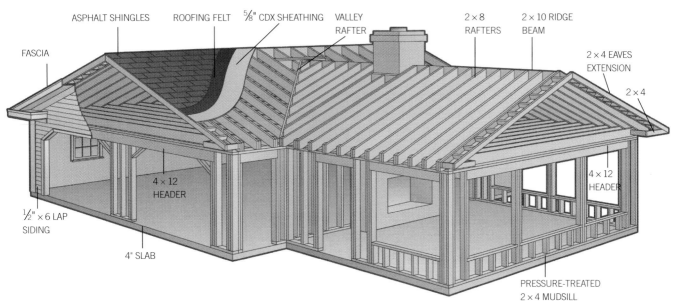

FASCIA

ASPHALT SHINGLES   ROOFING FELT   ⅝" CDX SHEATHING   VALLEY RAFTER   2 × 8 RAFTERS   2 × 10 RIDGE BEAM

2 × 4 EAVES EXTENSION

2 × 4

4 × 12 HEADER

4 × 12 HEADER

½" × 6 LAP SIDING

4" SLAB

PRESSURE-TREATED 2 × 4 MUDSILL

DESIGN DETAILS

Looking for nothing grander than a two-car gable garage? Then leave off the fireplace and the addition to this well-constructed 24-foot × 38-foot structure. Either way, the walls are stick-framed with 2 × 4s and the roof is stick-framed with 2 × 8s; the roof pitch is 8 in 12.

If you do decide to go with the added space of the summer room, consider hiring a pro to frame just the roof—intersecting roof lines are about as challenging as hip roof framing. You'll also want to hire a mason to build the fireplace box and chimney.

The interior of the summer room can be insulated and finished with drywall; in temperate climates, you may want to leave the studs bare for a true summer-cottage effect.

MATERIALS LIST

NAME	DIMENSIONS
Crushed stone, rebar, welded wire mesh, concrete for T-shaped slab foundation and for optional chimney footing	
Rigid insulation for frost protection of slab	¾"
Brick and mortar for chimney	
Pressure-treated mudsill	2 × 4
Plates, wall studs, eaves extensions	2 × 4
Headers, rafters, and collar ties	2 × 6
Trim, rafters	2 × 8
Headers, ridge beam, ceiling joists in garage	2 × 10
Headers for overhead doors, summer room	4 × 12
CDX wall and roof sheathing	⅝"
Drip edge, flashing, 15-lb. roofing felt, shakes	
Lap siding	½" × 6"
Vapor retarder	
Overhead doors	7' 0" × 9' 0"
Prehung double door, door set	6' 0" × 6' 8"
Prehung entry door, door set	3' 0" × 6' 8"
Prehung entry doors, door sets	2' 8" × 6' 8"
Prehung interior door, door set	3' 0" × 6' 8"
3-unit combination windows	20" × 72"
Double-hung window	26" × 41"
Double-hung windows	32" × 57"
Corner trim and fascia	1 × 8
Soffit	1 × 6
Crown molding and bed molding for trim	
Galvanized nails and outdoor screws	
Metal post anchors, metal framing brackets, soffit vent, and fasteners	
Paint, stain, or wood preservative	

HOW TO BUILD A TWO-CAR GABLE ROOF GARAGE

When two roof lines meet (as in the roofs of the garage and the summer room), the intersection is called a valley. Valleys are typically supported by a valley rafter that extends from the outside wall of the extended area to the ridge board or header. Because these valley rafters support considerable weight under snow load, they should be engineered for your locale.

1 Pour the Foundation

Excavate for the T-shaped foundation, install #4 rebar around the perimeter trench, and build forms. Add a layer of crushed stone, and pour concrete for the footings (see pages 98–99 for more on footings and foundations). When that's cured, pour the concrete for the slab and the footing for the optional chimney (see the floor plan, below). Level and smooth the concrete. Then locate anchor positions for the mudsills, and install them in the still-wet concrete. To cure the concrete, cover it with plastic sheeting and keep the slab damp for two to three days.

2 Frame the Walls

Cut 2 × 4 pressure-treated mudsills for the perimeter. Transfer anchor locations to the sill, and drill holes for the bolts to pass through. Cut top plates to match the mudsills, and lay out wall studs (see pages 101 and 104) 16 inches on center on pairs of mudsills/top plates. Lay out rough openings for the windows, the doors, and the overhead garage doors. Cut wall studs to 96 inches and build the walls in sections. Add jack studs, 2 × 10 and 4 × 12 headers, cripple studs, and sills as required.

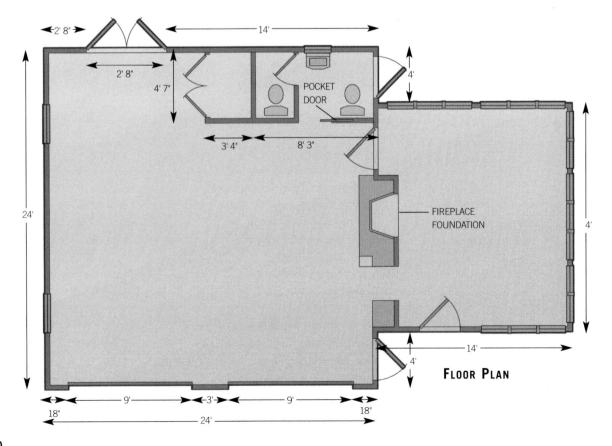

FLOOR PLAN

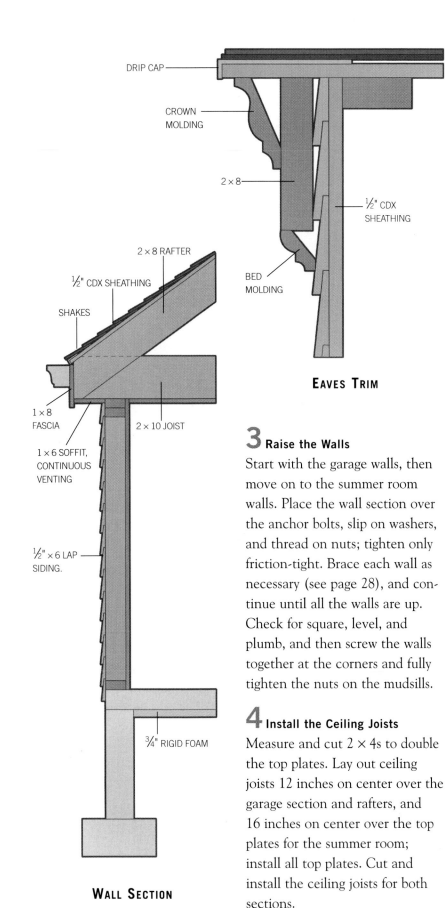

DRIP CAP

CROWN MOLDING

2 × 8

½" CDX SHEATHING

BED MOLDING

EAVES TRIM

2 × 8 RAFTER

½" CDX SHEATHING

SHAKES

1 × 8 FASCIA

2 × 10 JOIST

1 × 6 SOFFIT, CONTINUOUS VENTING

½" × 6 LAP SIDING.

¾" RIGID FOAM

WALL SECTION

5 Frame the Roof

Start framing the roof by cutting a 2 × 10 ridge board to length for the garage section. Then make a rafter template and cut rafters to length. Attach pairs of rafters to the ends of the ridge board and lift onto the garage; attach with rafter ties. Install the remaining rafters, except for those on the side where the summer room roof will attach. Then cut and install a doubled header to attach the ridge board of the summer roof (13 feet above the floor). Cut and install supporting jack studs. Cut and install the ridge board and rafters for the summer room roof. Then cut and attach the 2 × 4 eaves extensions. Sheath the roof frame with ⅝-inch CDX, add drip edge and 15-pound roofing felt, and cover with asphalt shingles. Then add the ridge caps. (Note: If you're installing a fireplace, make sure to leave an opening for the chimney and have the chimney installed by a mason before you add flashing and shingles.)

3 Raise the Walls

Start with the garage walls, then move on to the summer room walls. Place the wall section over the anchor bolts, slip on washers, and thread on nuts; tighten only friction-tight. Brace each wall as necessary (see page 28), and continue until all the walls are up. Check for square, level, and plumb, and then screw the walls together at the corners and fully tighten the nuts on the mudsills.

4 Install the Ceiling Joists

Measure and cut 2 × 4s to double the top plates. Lay out ceiling joists 12 inches on center over the garage section and rafters, and 16 inches on center over the top plates for the summer room; install all top plates. Cut and install the ceiling joists for both sections.

6 Add the Siding

Enclose the walls by first installing ⅝-inch CDX sheathing. Cover this with a vapor retarder, and install the windows and doors. Add continuous-soffit vent, 2 × 8 trim, 1 × 8 corner trim and fascia, and crown and bed molding to the eaves. Complete the structure by cutting and installing the beveled siding.

three-car reverse-gable garage

Need more elbowroom? And car, boat, workshop, and storage room? Steer toward this spacious garage. A cedar shake roof and cedar siding provide maintenance-free protection for the great indoors: 24 feet by 32 feet. Skylights help the side windows bring in light; the third bay helps you spread out.

Even for households without three cars, a three-bay garage can make a lot of sense: It provides plenty of coveted storage space. If your lot permits, expanding from a two-car plan to a three-car can be remarkably cost-effective.

DESIGN: GARAGES, ETC.

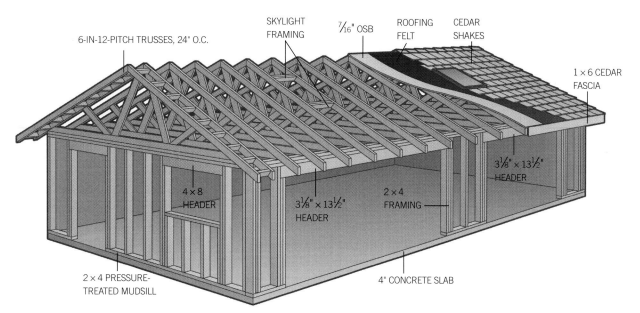

6-IN-12-PITCH TRUSSES, 24" O.C.

SKYLIGHT FRAMING

$\frac{7}{16}$" OSB

ROOFING FELT

CEDAR SHAKES

1 × 6 CEDAR FASCIA

$3\frac{1}{8}$" × $13\frac{1}{2}$" HEADER

4 × 8 HEADER

$3\frac{1}{8}$" × $13\frac{1}{2}$" HEADER

2 × 4 FRAMING

2 × 4 PRESSURE-TREATED MUDSILL

4" CONCRETE SLAB

DESIGN DETAILS

The walls of this three-car reverse-gable garage are stick-framed and the roof is framed with pre-engineered trusses; trusses can be ordered at most full-service lumberyards. A pair of skylights on the front of the roof bring in natural daylight, which is a real plus if you plan to use a portion of the garage for a work-shop or other activity center. This design is easy to modify to a one- or two-car garage simply by short-ening the width of the structure.

MATERIALS LIST

NAME	DIMENSIONS
Pea gravel and concrete for slab foundation	
Rebar	#4
Pressure-treated mudsills	2 × 4
Plates, wall/cripple studs eaves extensions	2 × 4
Window headers	4 × 8
Laminated veneer lumber door headers	$3\frac{1}{8}$"× $13\frac{1}{2}$"
Cedar door wrap	2 × 6
Skylight framing	2 × 6
Cedar fascia	1 × 6
Cedar corner boards and window wrap	1 × 4
Cedar trim	1 × 2
OSB wall sheathing	$\frac{7}{16}$"
Vapor retarder	
CDX roof sheathing	$\frac{1}{2}$"
Skylights	2' 0" × 4' 0"
Prehung door	3' 0" × 6' 8"
Sliding window	5' 0" × 3' 0"
Preengineered trusses with 6 in 12 slope	
Cedar medium-shake roofing	#1
Cedar ridge caps	
Cedar lap siding	8"
Cedar channel siding	8"
Overhead door	9' × 7'
Overhead door	16' × 7'
Galvanized nails and outdoor screws	
Metal post anchors	
Metal framing brackets and fasteners	
Door set	
Paint, stain, or wood preservative	

HOW TO BUILD A THREE-CAR REVERSE GABLE GARAGE

In keeping with the cedar siding and shake roofing, the rough openings of the doors and windows for this garage are "wrapped" with cedar. The door openings are wrapped with cedar 2 × 6s, and the window openings with cedar 1 × 4s. If you're not planning on using cedar siding and don't want to add the window and door wrap, then don't frame the rough openings larger, as explained in Step 2.

1 Pour the Foundation

Excavate for the slab foundation, install #4 rebar around the perimeter trench, and build forms. Add a layer of pea gravel or crushed stone; pour the concrete. Level and smooth the concrete. Locate anchor positions for the mudsills; install them in the still-wet concrete. Cover with plastic and keep damp two to three days.

2 Frame the Walls

Once the concrete has cured, remove the plastic wrap and cut 2 × 4 pressure-treated mudsills for the perimeter. Transfer anchor locations, and drill holes for the bolts. Cut top plates to match the mudsills, and lay out wall studs 16 inches on center on pairs of mudsills/top plates. Lay out rough openings as well for the left side window and for the door and the overhead doors. (Note: Overhead door rough openings are framed 1½ inches higher and 3 inches wider than normal to allow for the addition of 2 × 6 cedar door wrap.) Cut sufficient studs to 96 inches, and build the walls in sections. Add jack studs, headers, cripple studs, and sills as required.

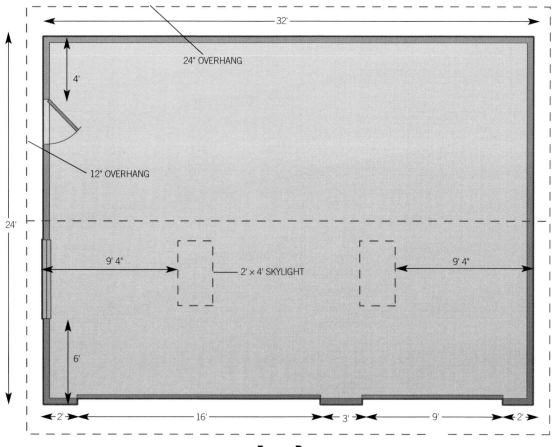

FLOOR PLAN

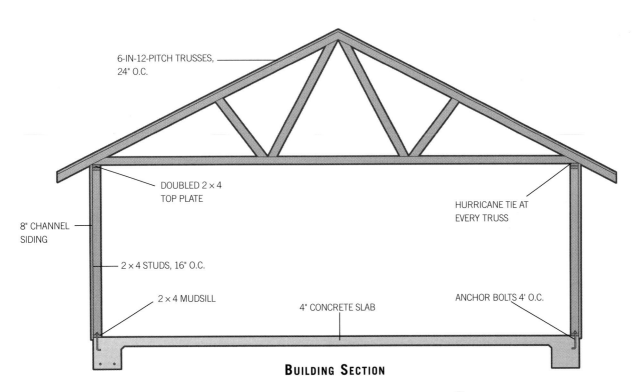

6-IN-12-PITCH TRUSSES, 24" O.C.

DOUBLED 2 × 4 TOP PLATE

8" CHANNEL SIDING

HURRICANE TIE AT EVERY TRUSS

2 × 4 STUDS, 16" O.C.

2 × 4 MUDSILL

4" CONCRETE SLAB

ANCHOR BOLTS 4' O.C.

BUILDING SECTION

3 Raise the Walls

Starting with the sides, place the wall section over the anchor bolts, slip on washers, and thread on nuts; tighten only friction-tight. Brace each wall as necessary and continue until all four walls are up. Check for square, level, and plumb, then screw the walls together at the corners and fully tighten the nuts on the mudsills. Then cut double top plates, mark the truss locations every 24 inches on center on the eaves plates, and install the double top plates.

4 Frame the Roof

Preengineered trusses let you skip the often challenging task of cutting rafters. Lift the end trusses up onto the walls and, with the aid of a couple of helpers, swing an end truss up into the upright position and secure it flush with the double top plates. Brace as needed. Add the remaining trusses 24 inches on center, bracing as you go and then frame for the skylights. Then cut and install the gable eaves extensions—these pieces are cut just like rafters of the trusses. This "ladder" is then attached to the end trusses to extend out past the gable ends.

5 Install Skylights, Add Roofing

If you're going to add skylights, add 2 × 6 blocking or "curb" between the trusses as shown on the floor plan. Next, sheath the roof with ⅞₆-inch OSB (oriented-strand board) or plywood. Cover the sheathing with 15-pound roofing felt, install the skylights and recommended flashing, and then attach cedar shake roofing and ridge caps.

6 Install Trim

Cut and install 1 × 6 cedar fascia, 1 × 4 cedar corner boards and window wrap, and 1 × 2 cedar window trim. Install the overhead doors now, or have them installed professionally.

7 Apply the Siding

Enclose the walls by attaching sheets of ⅞₆-inch OSB or plywood to the studs and top and bottom plates. Install the left-side window and door in the rough openings; then cover the sheathing with a vapor retarder. Attach 8-inch cedar channel siding vertically to the front and back walls and up to the top plates on the gable ends. Apply 8-inch lap siding horizontally above the channel siding on the gable ends.

small gable barn

Compact size and colonial styling merge in a small barn that's big on flexibility. Use the entire 10-foot by 16-foot interior for storage, or divvy it up for storage plus playroom (or office, or workspace). Easy to build, this model offers double doors on the side and gable end for ready access.

Like any gable-roofed structure, this barn is stretchable. If you need a wider entryway or more interior space, simply alter the plan and lengthen the barn. This design includes a row of transom windows (see cutaway view opposite)—a great way to enhance interior illumination. (To buy this shed in kit form, see page 160.)
DESIGN: BETTER BARNS.

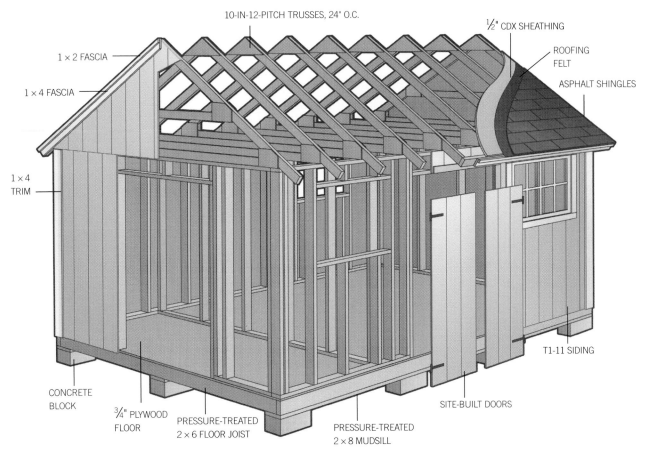

10-IN-12-PITCH TRUSSES, 24" O.C.

1 × 2 FASCIA

1 × 4 FASCIA

½" CDX SHEATHING

ROOFING FELT

ASPHALT SHINGLES

1 × 4 TRIM

T1-11 SIDING

CONCRETE BLOCK

¾" PLYWOOD FLOOR

PRESSURE-TREATED 2 × 6 FLOOR JOIST

PRESSURE-TREATED 2 × 8 MUDSILL

SITE-BUILT DOORS

DESIGN DETAILS

Given its beefy 10-foot by 16-foot size, this 2 × 4 stick-framed barn is very easy to build. The roofing is simplified with 2 × 4 trusses that you make at the site. The siding is T1-11, which is quick and easy to install.

The barn described here is built on concrete blocks on a pea-gravel base. Make sure to check with your local building inspector to see if this is allowed in your area. If you need to use poured footings, see pages 98–100.

MATERIALS LIST

NAME	DIMENSIONS
Pea gravel and concrete blocks or piers for foundation	
Concrete patio blocks as needed to level	
Pressure-treated mudsills	2 × 8
Pressure-treated floor framing	2 × 6
Tongue-and-groove plywood flooring	¾"
T1-11 exterior sheathing	⅝"
CDX roof sheathing and gussets	½"
Plates, studs, headers, cripple studs and sills, trusses, and sub-fascia	2 × 4
Barn sash windows	2' 0" × 3' 0"
Tongue-and-groove cedar door and door bracing	1 × 6
Cedar fascia, corner, window and door trim	1 × 2, 1 × 4
Drip edge and 15-lb. roofing felt	
Asphalt shingles and ridge caps	
Galvanized nails and outdoor screws	
Metal framing brackets and fasteners	
Strap hinges and door latch	
Paint, stain, or wood preservative	

HOW TO BUILD A SMALL GABLE BARN

Once you've got the floor for this small barn framed and covered, consider jumping a step ahead and fabricating the roof trusses. Lay these out directly on the floor and attach cleats to the floor to serve as stops for the pieces. Then you can quickly build the trusses assembly-line-style and then set them aside until after you've framed the walls.

1 Install the Foundation

The foundation for this shed can be concrete piers, blocks, or poured footings (see pages 98–99 for more on foundations). Start by leveling the area, laying out an 11-foot × 17-foot rectangle, and excavating 4 inches of soil. Fill this with 4 inches of pea gravel for drainage. Then place twelve 4 × 8 × 16 concrete blocks in three rows spaced 59 inches apart. Find the high point and shim the blocks level, using patio blocks.

2 Frame the Floor

The floor is framed with 2 × 6 pressure-treated lumber that attaches to 2 × 8 mudsills (or runners) that rest on the concrete blocks. To frame the floor, first create a front and rear rim joist by nailing a 2 × 6 to a 2 × 8 mudsill; cut a third mudsill to fit on top of center blocks. Then lay out floor joists 16 inches on center (see page 101). Place mudsills on top of blocks, and cut 2 × 6 joists to

a length of 117 inches and insert them between rim joists; secure with 16d nails or joist hangers. Cover the floor frame with ¾-inch tongue-and-groove plywood, and secure it with 8d galvanized nails.

3 Build the Walls

To begin on the wall sections, start by cutting the top and bottom plates: You'll need four front/back wall plates at 9 feet 10 inches and four side wall plates at 9 feet 5 inches. Lay out wall studs every 16 inches on center (see pages 27–28 and 104) and locate rough openings. The windows are 14½ inches in from wall ends, and the opening is 36¼ inches wide and 25¼ inches high; the bottom of the header is 72 inches up from floor. The 58- × 72-inch door opening is centered on the front wall. Place studs between the top/bottom plates and secure with 16d nails; add headers, sills, and cripple studs as needed.

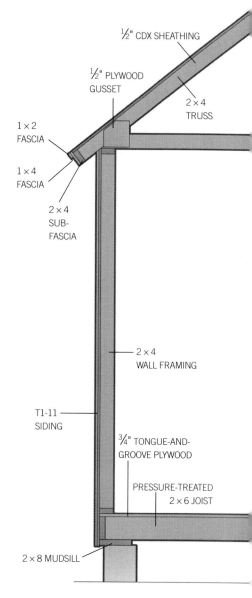

½" CDX SHEATHING

½" PLYWOOD GUSSET

2 × 4 TRUSS

1 × 2 FASCIA

1 × 4 FASCIA

2 × 4 SUB-FASCIA

2 × 4 WALL FRAMING

T1-11 SIDING

¾" TONGUE-AND-GROOVE PLYWOOD

PRESSURE-TREATED 2 × 6 JOIST

2 × 8 MUDSILL

WALL SECTION

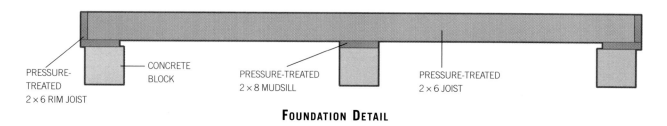

PRESSURE-TREATED 2 × 6 RIM JOIST

CONCRETE BLOCK

PRESSURE-TREATED 2 × 8 MUDSILL

PRESSURE-TREATED 2 × 6 JOIST

FOUNDATION DETAIL

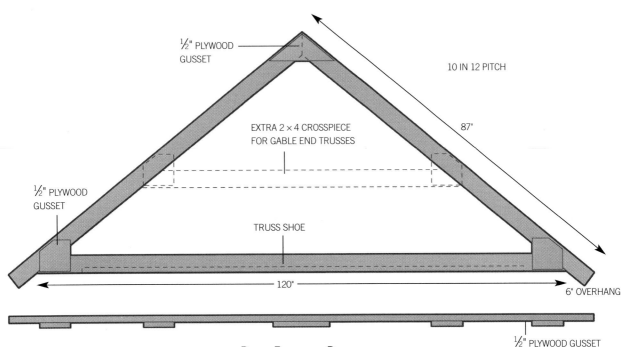

½" PLYWOOD GUSSET

EXTRA 2 × 4 CROSSPIECE FOR GABLE END TRUSSES

10 IN 12 PITCH

87"

½" PLYWOOD GUSSET

TRUSS SHOE

120"

6" OVERHANG

½" PLYWOOD GUSSET

ROOF FRAMING DETAIL

4 Raise the Walls

Lift each wall section into position and secure it to the floor with 3-inch deck screws; brace as needed (see page 28). Raise the remaining walls; when they're square, level, and plumb, screw the corners of the walls together. If you're planning on adding an internal wall partition, build and install it at this point.

5 Frame the Roof

Roof framing is simplified with trusses. Each truss is made up of two 2 × 4 rafters and one 2 × 4 ceiling joist joined together with plywood gussets (see the truss detail, above). The easiest way to build these is to lay out rafters on the shed floor and build the trusses there. Cut the rafters to length with a 40-degree angle cut at one end. Cut the gussets and cross braces to size. Make a template on the shed floor and position stop blocks to hold the parts in place while you attach gussets. Note that the gable end trusses have an extra cross brace to serve as a nailer for the gable siding.

6 Add the Siding to the Gables

Attach T1-11 sheathing to gable end trusses, and attach these to the top plates of the gable end walls. Install the remaining trusses, one over each wall stud, bracing them as needed; secure with 3-inch deck screws. Cover the trusses with ½-inch CDX plywood, and cut and attach subfascia, fascia, and trim per the wall section shown opposite. Install drip edge, cover with 15-pound felt paper, and install asphalt shingles and ridge caps. (See pages 113 and 115 for more on roofing options.)

7 Side the Walls

Enclose the walls with T1-11 exterior sheathing. Add trim around the window or door openings and at the corners of the barn to cover the exposed edges of the siding. Use 2-foot × 3-foot barn sash for the windows, and make simple frames to accept them; they're held closed at the top with a barrel bolt.

The transom window is a 5-foot-long 1 × 4 ladder frame backed by a single pane of glass. The doors are built from 1 × 6 tongue-and-groove cedar and battens cut from 1-by stock; attach the battens with 1½-inch screws, and hang doors with heavy-duty strap hinges.

horse barn

Corral some serious space in this handsome, sturdy horse barn that adapts to multiple needs. At 30 feet by 50 feet, it accommodates eight horse stalls, a hayloft, and accessory rooms. Or, transform it into the ultimate workshop. A roof pitched to shed water and snow well will shelter anything you have in mind.

Build the wall sections, gather your friends, and host a barn raising. This timber-framed structure breaks the job down into doable stages without the complicated mortise-and-tenon joints of traditional barns. This is a major project—you may want to hire pros for most of the structure and complete the detailing yourself. DESIGN: GROFFDALE BARNS.

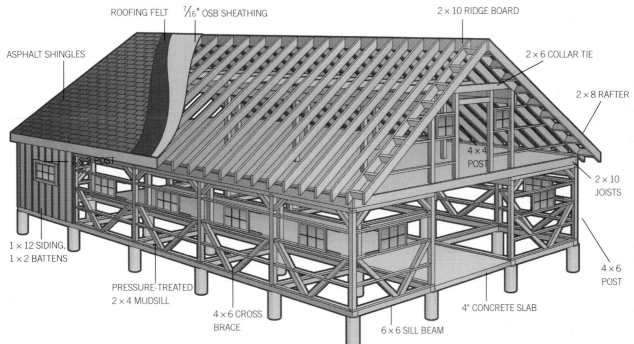

ROOFING FELT
7/16" OSB SHEATHING
2 × 10 RIDGE BOARD
ASPHALT SHINGLES
2 × 6 COLLAR TIE
2 × 8 RAFTER
4 × 4 POST
2 × 3 POST
2 × 10 JOISTS
1 × 12 SIDING, 1 × 2 BATTENS
4 × 6 POST
PRESSURE-TREATED 2 × 4 MUDSILL
4 × 6 CROSS BRACE
6 × 6 SILL BEAM
4" CONCRETE SLAB

DESIGN DETAILS

Professional barn builders pre-fabricate as much of the barn as possible and then assemble the barn on site. They deliver two 9-foot-square, 50-foot-long stall sections and attach these to concrete footings. Next they connect the two sections with ceiling joists, add a floor, and then frame the roof. They then fill the ground floor section between the stalls with concrete and cover the openings at each end with sliding doors. You can use a similar technique by building the walls on site.

MATERIALS LIST

NAME	DIMENSIONS
Pea gravel and concrete for poured footings	
Steel angle plate and anchors	3/16"
Welded wire mesh and concrete for center slab	
Pressure-treated mudsills	2 × 4
Oak top plates	2 × 4
Oak corner posts and bracing	4 × 6
Oak posts for second floor	4 × 4
Spruce headers, joists	2 × 8
Spruce headers and ridge board	2 × 10
Sill beams	6 × 6
Collar ties	2 × 6
Tongue-and-groove planks for stall fronts	2 × 8
Oak kickboards for stalls	1 × 8
OSB roof sheathing	7/16"
CDX tongue-and-groove flooring	5/8"
Drip edge, 15-lb. roofing felt, asphalt shingles	
Sliding doors, latches	5' 0" × 8' 0"
Interior door, hinges, door set	3' 0" × 6' 8"
Hayloft doors, latches	4' 0" × 7' 0"
6-light barn sashes for stalls	32"
6-light barn sashes	36"
4-light barn sashes for hayloft	24"
Sliding doors with box track for stalls	4' 0"
White pine soffit and fascia	
White pine siding, battens	1 × 12, 1 × 2
Galvanized nails, outdoor screws, metal framing brackets	
Paint, stain, or wood preservative	

HOW TO BUILD A HORSE BARN

The strength of the structure comes from the heavy beams and the board-and-batten siding. Do not use alternate siding without reengineering the framing. Also, oak parts must be used for the frame pieces: Pine is not strong enough, and the structure would have to be reengineered. The roof pitch is 9 in 12.

1 Install the Foundation

On such a large, heavy structure, it's important that the weight transfers to the footings. That's why all the vertical support beams are positioned directly over the concrete piers (see foundation detail, right). The stall sections rest on 6 × 6 beams that run along the central open area inside the barn; use ship-lap joints at the corners, and bolt the corners together with ½-inch carriage bolts. These 6 × 6s span the piers (see floor plan, below). Attach the beams to the concrete footings with 5-inch × 5-inch ³⁄₁₆-inch-thick angle plates and bolts.

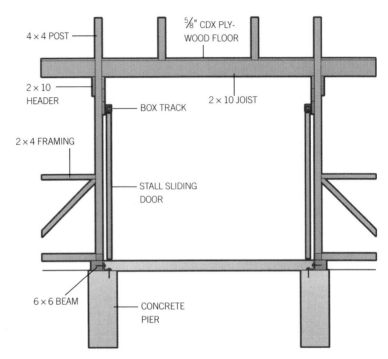

4 × 4 POST

⅝" CDX PLY-WOOD FLOOR

2 × 10 HEADER

BOX TRACK

2 × 10 JOIST

2 × 4 FRAMING

STALL SLIDING DOOR

6 × 6 BEAM

CONCRETE PIER

FOUNDATION DETAIL

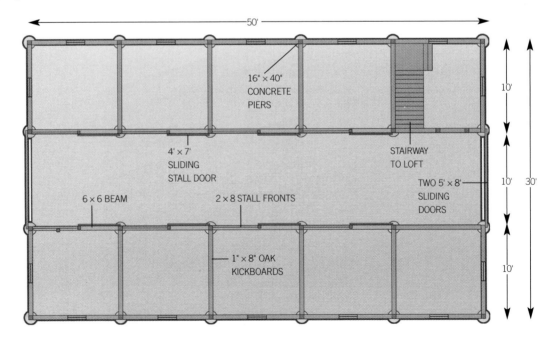

50'

16" × 40" CONCRETE PIERS

4' × 7' SLIDING STALL DOOR

STAIRWAY TO LOFT

6 × 6 BEAM

2 × 8 STALL FRONTS

TWO 5' × 8' SLIDING DOORS

1" × 8" OAK KICKBOARDS

10'

10'

10'

30'

FLOOR PLAN

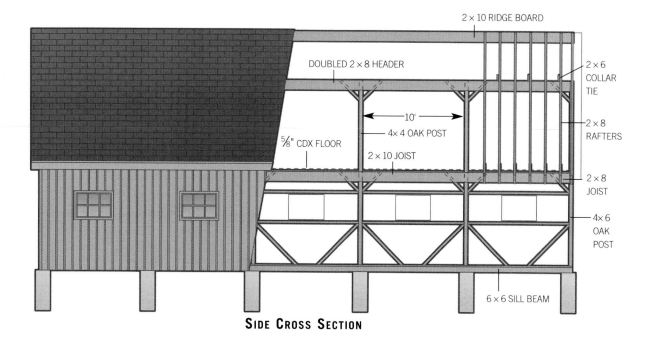

2 × 10 RIDGE BOARD

DOUBLED 2 × 8 HEADER

2 × 6 COLLAR TIE

2 × 8 RAFTERS

10'

4× 4 OAK POST

⅝" CDX FLOOR

2 × 10 JOIST

2 × 8 JOIST

4× 6 OAK POST

6 × 6 SILL BEAM

SIDE CROSS SECTION

Reinforce the center section between the stall beams with welded wire mesh and pour a concrete slab foundation. (Note: Horse stalls are often left with dirt floors; you can pour concrete in these if desired.)

2 Frame the Walls

Each side of a stall section consists of a 4 × 4 top plate, which rests on 4 × 6 posts in each corner, and 4 × 4 posts along the length of the wall; these posts rest on 2 × 4 mudsills (see side cross section, above). Three horizontal 2 × 4 cross bracing/nailing boards span the posts and are spaced an equal distance apart; there's also 4 × 4 diagonal cross bracing near the top of each post and from the posts to the mudsill at the bottom (see wall section on page 94). After these pieces are nailed together, square the frames and attach vertical board-and-batten siding on the exterior (1 × 12

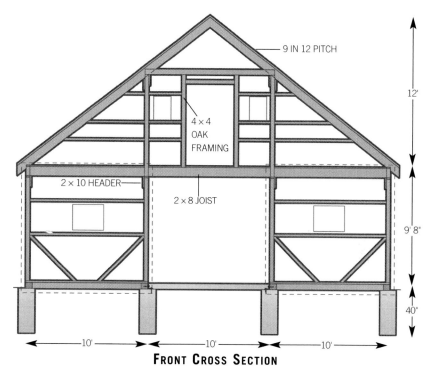

9 IN 12 PITCH

12'

4 × 4 OAK FRAMING

2 × 10 HEADER

2 × 8 JOIST

9' 8"

40"

10'   10'   10'

FRONT CROSS SECTION

boards and 1 × 2 battens); see the corner detail on page 94. Two 1 × 2 scraps are nailed to the top and middle cross bracing to serve as a track for the barn sash windows. This lets the window slide horizontally to open and close. The interior stall section walls are

framed in a similar manner, except horizontal tongue-and-groove pine siding is attached.

3 Raise the Walls

Because they are so large and heavy, raising the walls requires a lot of help, a crane, or a block

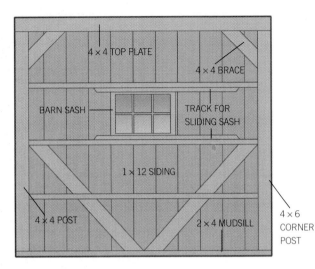

WALL SECTION

Labels: 4 × 4 TOP PLATE, 4 × 4 BRACE, BARN SASH, TRACK FOR SLIDING SASH, 1 × 12 SIDING, 4 × 4 POST, 2 × 4 MUDSILL, 4 × 6 CORNER POST

CORNER DETAIL

Labels: 1 × 2 BATTEN, 1 × 12 BOARD, 4 × 4, 4 × 4 BRACE, 16d GALVANIZED NAILS, 4 × 6 POST

and tackle. Position each wall on top of the 6 × 6 sill beams and secure it with nails; add temporary braces until the end walls can be raised. Cut and install 2 × 10 headers on inside tops of walls running the full length of the structure; then attach 2 × 10 headers to both top faces of interior walls. The headers help support the ceiling joist (see foundation detail on page 92). Then cut and install the 2 × 4 double top plates. Repeat this sequence for the second stall section.

4 Install the Ceiling Joists
Connect the two stall sections by running 2 × 8 ceiling joists every 16 inches on center. Attach them to the headers and walls. Install the rim joists to cover the ends. Then cut and install ⅝-inch or ¾-inch tongue-and-groove CDX plywood flooring. Build a set of stairs to the second floor or just make a simple wooden ladder to the loft.

5 Frame the Roof
The roof pitch is 9 in 12. To start framing, cut a 2 × 10 ridge board and secure it in place with temporary bracing. Make a rafter template and cut the 2 × 8 rafters to length (see page 114). Attach to the ridge board and double top plate; brace as needed. Cut and install 4 × 4 second floor posts 10 feet on center so they're directly over the posts on the ground floor. Cut and install the double header and secure it to posts and rafters (see header detail right). Build a pair of eaves extensions to bring the roof past the gable ends (see page 79). Cut and install the sub-fascia, fascia, and soffit. Cover the roof framing with ⁷⁄₁₆-inch sheathing; add drip edge and roofing felt, cover with asphalt shingles, and install ridge caps.

6 Frame the Floor
On the second floor, frame the gable ends as shown in the front cross section (page 93). Create a

rough opening on each end for a door and two windows; add top cross bracing as per a standard wall. Cut and install board-and-batten siding to cover gable ends.

7 Install Door and Windows
Add barn sash to the wall partitions, and build a pair of board-and-batten doors for the hayloft. Cut and install simple trim around windows and doors. Cover interior walls if desired, and add sliding doors to the stalls.

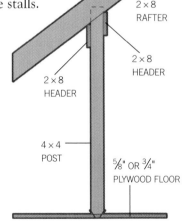

Labels: 2 × 8 RAFTER, 2 × 8 HEADER, 2 × 8 HEADER, 4 × 4 POST, ⅝" OR ¾" PLYWOOD FLOOR

HEADER DETAIL

construction know-how

A SHED IS AN IDEAL PROJECT for a budding carpenter. And while a garage or barn is more demanding (particularly of the friends and family members you'll need as helpers), each allows a reasonable margin of error compared to residential remodeling projects. Best of all, these projects happen outdoors, where the havoc of construction won't disrupt daily life. ▪ In addition to fastening and cutting skills (especially the safe and accurate use of a circular saw), you will need to be comfortable making precise measurements and checking, again and again, that your work is level and plumb. You'll also need to know how to use a framing square and a handy technique called the "3-4-5 triangle" (see page 103) for the important task of checking that your work is square. ▪ Whether exploring new techniques or refreshing old skills, you'll find that this chapter offers the essential construction know-how for successfully completing your shed, garage, or barn.

tools

WATER LEVEL

25-FOOT TAPE MEASURE

SPEED SQUARE

TORPEDO LEVEL

CHALK LINE

FRAMING SQUARE

4-FOOT LEVEL

PLUMB BOB

LINE LEVEL

One of the most critical steps in building a new structure is measuring and laying out the project, particularly the foundation. To do this with precision, you'll need a 25-foot tape measure for general-purpose measuring (for larger structures, you'll want a 50-foot reel tape as well). To lay out the site and check for right angles, buy a framing square plus a speed square (also handy for marking framing cuts).

To check that things are on a true horizontal (level) or true vertical (plumb), have on hand a 4-foot level, a torpedo level, and a line level. You may also need a water level for leveling points across a long distance, and a post level to check framing. Buy a chalk line for striking layout lines, and a plumb bob to transfer location points for footings and piers.

HAND TOOLS

In addition to measuring and layout tools, basic framing and construction requires a claw hammer, a hand saw for completing plunge cuts and trimming parts, and a compass saw for cutting notches in framing members and flooring. You'll also need a utility knife, a wood chisel, and a block plane for fine-tuning the fit of parts. Grab a pry bar, too—it's handy for levering and for undoing mistakes. Buy tin snips for cutting sheet metal, and a ratchet and socket set for tightening nuts and bolts. As you finish the job, use a caulk gun for applying caulk around trim.

For digging, you'll need a spade shovel; a manual post-hole digger (often called a clamshell digger) or, better yet, a power auger (see Specialty Tools opposite and page 100). Also have on hand a wheelbarrow, a hoe, and a masonry trowel or two.

POWER TOOLS

Power tools can make quick work of many of the tedious tasks involved in building a new structure. Use an electric drill with a ½-inch chuck for large-diameter holes—even for mixing joint compound. A cordless driver/drill with a ⅜-inch chuck is ideal for drilling smaller holes and driving screws.

Depending on your structure, you may also need a right-angle

WOOD CHISEL

HAND SAW

UTILITY KNIFE

CLAW HAMMER

COMPASS SAW

PRY BAR

TIN SNIPS

CAULKING GUN

BLOCK PLANE

drill for working in tight spots, and a hammer drill with a masonry bit for drilling into concrete.

Useful power cutting tools include a circular saw for straight-square cuts, a reciprocating saw for cutting out window and door openings in sheathing as well as cutting through sill plates at doors, and a saber saw for cutting access holes and curves. In addition, a power miter saw, or "chop saw," is the best choice for accurately cutting framing members to length with precision. A miter saw can also pivot to make precise angled cuts for trim. Consider renting one of these tools for a day or two if you don't own one.

CIRCULAR SAW

CORDLESS DRILL

POWER MITER SAW

DRILL WITH ½" CHUCK

RIGHT-ANGLE DRILL

SABER SAW

RECIPROCATING SAW

HAMMER DRILL

SAFETY GEAR

As with any home improvement project, it's important to protect yourself by wearing appropriate safety gear. Use protective head-gear for working in tight quarters and with overhead framing mem-bers. Wear leather gloves when working with concrete or hefting lumber. Put on safety goggles any-time your work might send dust and debris flying, and always wear ear protectors when working with power tools.

A dust mask or respirator will protect your lungs from sawdust (particularly the toxic dust from pressure-treated lumber). Finally, this kind of work involves a lot of kneeling. You'll appreciate a pair of knee pads.

HELPERS

The challenge of building a shed, garage, or barn isn't cutting and nailing or screwing all the parts together—the real work is hefting heavy wood slabs and beams. A typical 12-foot pressure-treated 2 × 8 weighs more than 100 pounds. Multiply this by the 20 or so joists you have to install, and it can add up to a long day and a sore back. That's why it's best to enlist a helper or two when it's time to move timbers around.

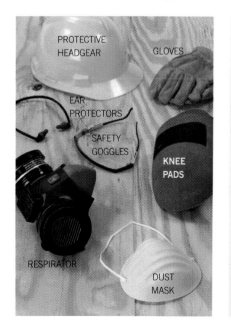

PROTECTIVE HEADGEAR

GLOVES

EAR PROTECTORS

SAFETY GOGGLES

KNEE PADS

RESPIRATOR

DUST MASK

SPECIALTY TOOLS

If you're planning to dig holes for concrete footings, consider renting a power auger. These gas-powered machines resemble a giant auger drill and will quickly excavate a lot of soil. If you have more than a bag or so of concrete to mix, you can rent a portable cement mixer which will quickly do the job with minimal effort. Cement mixers are either gas- or electric-powered. If you rent an electric mixer, guard against shock by plugging it into a GFCI (Ground Fault Circuit Interrupter) receptacle.

foundations

A small shed can get by with only a pair of skids (shown below) or a set of pre-cast concrete piers (shown right) as a foundation. However, a larger shed requires a more permanent foundation with the structure attached to a concrete footing. Owing to their size and weight, garages and barns are best built on slab foundations; see slab options on the opposite page.

USE JOIST HANGERS, OR NAIL RIM JOISTS TO JOISTS

¾" PLYWOOD FLOOR

PRECAST CONCRETE PIER

4" LAYER OF PEA GRAVEL FOR DRAINAGE

USE JOIST HANGERS, OR NAIL RIM JOISTS TO JOISTS

¾" PLYWOOD FLOOR

4 × 6 SKID

4" LAYER OF PEA GRAVEL

LANDSCAPE CLOTH

TEMPORARY FOUNDATIONS

A skid foundation is the easiest to construct and move—the skids allow you to tow the shed to a new location if desired. The skids are typically made of pressure-treated 4 × 6s with the ends tapered to keep them from digging into the ground when moved. Although the skids are pressure-treated, it's best to provide ample drainage to prevent rot. Good drainage also lessens the likelihood of soil eroding under a skid, causing the shed to tip. Excavate 4 inches of soil where the shed will be located. Then, to prevent weeds from

growing under the shed, apply a layer of landscape cloth. Cover this with 4 inches of pea gravel. Now you can build a 2 × 8 or 2 × 10 frame directly onto the skids and apply exterior-grade ¾-inch plywood for a solid floor.

Another way to make a temporary foundation is to use precast concrete piers. Some piers (like those shown, above right) have notches in their tops to accept dimensional lumber. Like a skid foundation, a pier foundation needs ample drainage to remain stable. You can excavate the entire area or just small squares around each pier, and fill in with pea gravel. The floor frame is built with

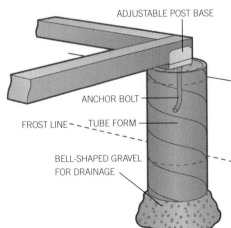

ADJUSTABLE POST BASE

ANCHOR BOLT

FROST LINE

TUBE FORM

BELL-SHAPED GRAVEL FOR DRAINAGE

2 × 12 rim joists as shown, then covered with ¾-inch exterior-grade plywood.

PERMANENT FOUNDATIONS

Permanent foundations can be poured footings, slabs, or a T-shaped foundation that combines features of both. Typically, slab or T-shaped foundations are reinforced with rebar and wire mesh to help prevent shifting and cracking.

POURED FOOTING A poured footing (below left) is the simplest permanent foundation and is ideal for small structures like sheds. (This type of foundation is commonly used for deck construction.) A poured footing is stable because its base rests below the frost line. Your local code will specify how deep the frost line is and how far below it you need to dig (usually 12 inches). Once the holes are dug with a post-hole digger or a power auger, you can use concrete tube forms to form the required footing. In most cases, code will require you to provide drainage by adding a layer of gravel below the footing.

The structure attaches to the footing with J-shaped anchor bolts embedded in the still-wet concrete. When dry, the metal post bases are attached to J-bolts to accept 4 × 4 posts that form the floor frame.

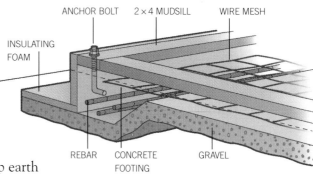

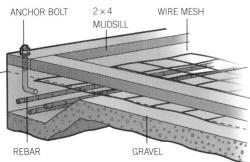

SLAB FOUNDATION An on-grade slab foundation (shown above) is used in warm climates where there's no danger of the ground freezing and thereby expanding and cracking the concrete. It's made of several inches of concrete cast on a bed of crushed gravel and reinforced with wire mesh or rebar. Slab on-grade foundations are fairly straightforward to install, although "floating" the surface level and smooth

requires special tools and skills.

FROST-PROTECTED FOUNDATION A frost-protected foundation uses sheets of rigid polystyrene insulation to keep earth beneath the concrete from freezing and heaving.

(as shown, above right) keeps the soil under a heated building from freezing. With an unheated building, sheet insulation can be placed under the entire slab.

T-SHAPED FOUNDATIONS Though now often supplanted by the simpler frost-protected slab foundation, a T-shaped foundation (right) is another alternative for structures built in cold climates. A T-shaped foundation consists of three main parts: a footing that extends below the frost line, founda-

tion walls that are centered over the footing, and a slab that runs between the walls. Footings are typically equal in depth to the width of the wall and twice as wide. Walls are made by pouring concrete into plywood forms. Wire mesh or rebar is embedded in the slab. Once the concrete is cured, the forms are removed.

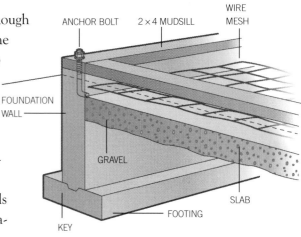

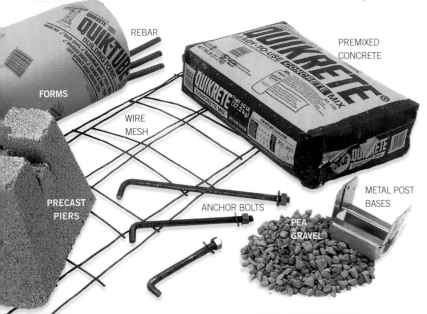

FOUNDATION MATERIALS
Foundations begin with a bed of pea gravel to provide drainage. Wooden or fiberglass forms hold and mold concrete for footings. Wire mesh or rebar reinforces concrete and helps prevent cracking. The concrete comes premixed in 50-pound bags (all you add is water). Precast concrete piers serve as footings for a temporary foundation. Anchor bolts are embedded in wet concrete and allow you to attach the structure; metal post bases attach to the anchor bolts and accept the framing members that make up the floor frame.

INSTALLING FOOTINGS

Although you can dig holes for poured footings with a post-hole digger, a power auger (below) will do the job faster and without the backache. Most rental centers carry these—when you rent one, have the salesperson explain its operation. Contact utilities (power, water, gas, telephone, and cable) to check for buried lines. Most areas require 48–72 hours' notice, so plan ahead. Call underground alert services at 800-642-2444 to see if they have information for your area. Caution: A power auger will kick when it bites into the dirt or hits a root or stone. Have a helper assist you in holding the auger.

If using a concrete tube form, cut it so it's 2 inches above grade when placed in the hole. Brace it with 2 × 4s attached with screws fastened from inside the tube.

Especially if you must dig numerous footings, a power auger saves time and spares your back.

1 Prepare the Concrete

Pour premixed concrete into a wheelbarrow and make a depression in the center. Add the recommended amount of clean water and mix using a mortar hoe, moving back and forth until all the water is absorbed by the mix.

2 Pour the Concrete

Move the wheelbarrow close to the hole. Use a spade to transfer the concrete into the hole. Have a helper tilt the wheelbarrow gently toward the hole. Direct the concrete with your shovel.

3 Release Trapped Air

Large air bubbles trapped in the concrete can weaken it. Use a thin scrap of wood to poke the concrete to release any trapped air. Level the footing by "screeding" the form with a wood scrap.

4 Install the Anchors

Locate each anchor's approximate position and push it into the concrete, wiggling slightly as you go to get the concrete to flow around the bolt. Use a torpedo level to check that it's level and plumb.

TIP: BUILD THE FRAME, THEN INSTALL THE ANCHOR

It's often tricky to locate anchors, especially if a foundation is less than perfectly square. This method lets you frame your floor, confirm anchor locations, then install them. Once the concrete cures, use a heavy-duty drill with a masonry bit to drill a hole for the bolt. Use an expansion bolt or set the anchor bolt with concrete epoxy.

framing and siding

Floor framing is attached directly to the foundation, beginning with the sill plate (sometimes called a mudsill). Although floor framing is fairly straightforward, it must be installed precisely; any imperfections will resonate into the walls and roof of the structure.

The sill plate lies flat on the foundation and is usually secured with evenly spaced metal anchor bolts. Drill larger holes than needed for the bolts so you can square up the sill plates using the 3-4-5 triangle method (page 103). Make adjustments as needed— the sill plates can extend slightly beyond the footing if necessary.

Install rim joists on top of the sill plate. These box in the joists, providing a frame for fastening them. Shim rim joists if they are not level. Floor joists typically span the distance from foundation wall to foundation wall. They are evenly spaced, their spacing and dimensions determined by local codes. The floor joists are covered with subflooring, usually ¾-inch tongue-and-groove plywood, or OSB (oriented-strand board).

Walls are built on top of the floor. A typical 2-by wall consists of vertical wall studs spaced 16 inches on center. These stand between the sole plate (attached to the subfloor) and the top plate (typically doubled, but on smaller structures a single 2 × 4).

Where an opening is made in the wall for a window or door, a horizontal framing member called a header is installed to assume the load of the wall studs that were removed. The header is supported by jack studs (also called trimmer studs) that are attached to full-length wall studs known as king studs. The shorter studs that run between the header and the top plate or from the underside of the rough sill of a window to the sole plate are called cripple studs.

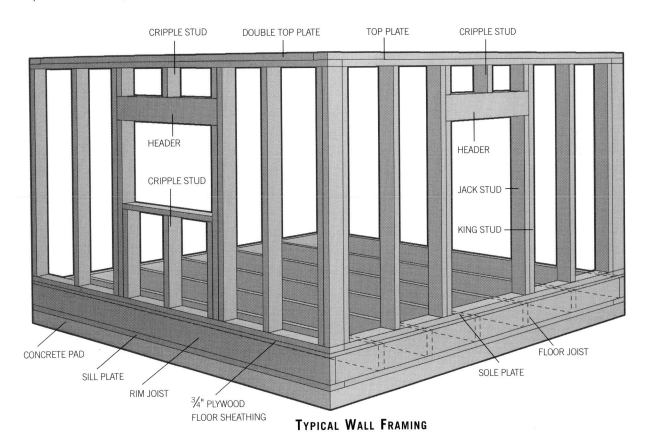

CRIPPLE STUD   DOUBLE TOP PLATE   TOP PLATE   CRIPPLE STUD

HEADER

CRIPPLE STUD

HEADER

JACK STUD

KING STUD

CONCRETE PAD

SILL PLATE

RIM JOIST

¾" PLYWOOD
FLOOR SHEATHING

FLOOR JOIST

SOLE PLATE

TYPICAL WALL FRAMING

REDWOOD

ALUMINUM

VINYL

T1-11 EXTERIOR PLYWOOD

CEDAR

HARDBOARD

SELECTING MATERIALS

For interior framing, wall studs are typically 2 × 4 or 2 × 6 and are usually SFP (Spruce-Fir-Pine). Douglas fir is often used for added strength for framing members that will be stressed, such as floor and ceiling joists, as well as rafters. For exposed framing members like floor joists, beams, and posts, consider pressure-treated lumber to resist damage from insects and moisture. Woods like redwood and western red cedar are naturally immune to these threats, but cost significantly more—and they're relatively soft and don't offer the strength of pine or fir.

CEDAR 4 × 4

2 × 6 DOUGLAS FIR

2 × 4 SPF

SHEATHING Sheathing is used to cover framing members. Floor sheathing has tongue-and-groove edges that interlock. Exterior wall sheathing is usually ½-inch- or ⅝-inch-thick plywood or OSB (oriented-strand board). Roof sheathing is most commonly ⅝-inch plywood. All sheathing should be span rated. This rating is part of the grade stamped on the sheathing. It's the recommended center-to-center spacing of supports, in inches, over which the panels should be installed. A span rating looks like a fraction (such as 32/16), but it isn't. The left number describes the maximum spacing of supports in inches when the panel is used for roof sheathing; the right number denotes the maximum support spacing when applied as subflooring.

SIDING Typical siding materials for sheds, garages, and barns include T1-11 exterior plywood,

OSB

EXTERIOR SHEATHING

TONGUE-AND-GROOVE PLYWOOD FLOOR SHEATHING

with its vertically spaced grooves; hardboard siding, available in a variety of widths; natural wood siding (usually redwood or cedar), either in the form of clapboard siding or shingles; and vinyl and metal siding that mimic clapboard siding and create a virtually maintenance-free exterior. (Metal and vinyl siding require special tools and are best installed by pros.)

FASTENERS Many building codes require metal framing fasteners where floor joists meet headers or rim joists, where studs meet sole plates, and so on. Check with your building inspector to identify what type of anchors (if any) are required in your area.

There are dozens of metal framing fasteners available to handle almost any situation. Joist hangers are the most common and are used to support a joist, girder, or other framing

GALVANIZED NAILS

SINKERS

FRAMING HARDWARE

CEMENT-COATED SINKERS

JOIST HANGER

COATED SCREWS

JOIST HANGER NAILS

member from a post, beam, rim joist, or header. They create a much stronger joint than would be possible by simply nailing framing members together. Note: For joist hangers to be able to reliably support their load, they must be installed with joist hanger nails. These specialized nails have a stout shank and increased shear strength.

For joining framing members unexposed to weather, use cement-coated sinkers. These are coated with a dry adhesive and won't later work their way out. Use hot-dipped galvanized nails or coated screws for applying siding and trim.

FRAMING TECHNIQUES

One of the best ways to ensure accuracy when framing is to make precise, straight cuts. To avoid dangerous binding, support long pieces of lumber in two places on both sides of the cut. For shorter pieces, use sawhorses and allow space for cutoffs to fall away. For repeat cuts, make simple jigs to quickly and accurately mark lumber.

SPEED SQUARE A speed square is an extremely handy tool for making accurate cuts with a circular saw. Place it on the workpiece so the lip of the square catches the edge of the workpiece. Butt the saw up against the adjacent edge of the square, and slide the saw and square so the blade is on the waste side of the marked line. Hold the square firmly in place as you push the saw through the cut, keeping the saw base in constant contact with the square.

FENCE AND STOP BLOCK Inaccurate cuts are common when cutting long boards on the miter saw. That's because the built-in fence is too short to fully support the board. To prevent this, attach a longer fence to the saw's built-in fence. Secure a long plywood fence to both sides of the built-in saw fence with screws. Now you can attach a stop block to the fence to make accurate repeat cuts. Firmly clamp

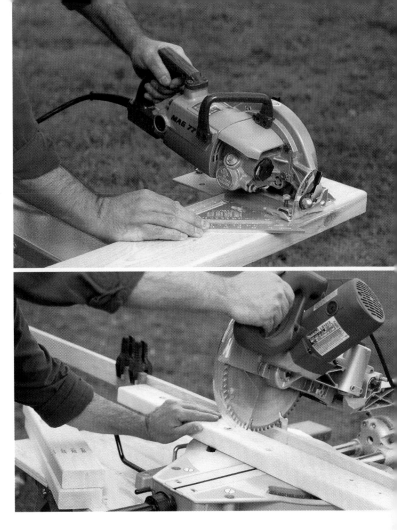

the stop to the fence so it's perpendicular to the saw table. Consider adding a strip of sandpaper to the face of the plywood fence. The sandpaper grit grips the wood and helps prevent it from creeping or shifting during a cut.

3-4-5 TRIANGLE

One of the oldest and most reliable ways to check adjacent legs of a corner for 90 degrees is to use a 3-4-5 triangle. To do this, measure and mark a point 3 feet from the centerpoint where the lines cross (make this mark on either line). Then measure and mark 4 feet from the centerpoint on the adjacent line. Now measure the distance from the 3-foot mark and the 4-foot mark with a tape measure (or a piece of string or wire rope). If the lines are perpendicular, the distance will measure exactly 5 feet. If it doesn't, the lines aren't perpendicular—adjust the position of one of the lines.

Enlist a helper when using this method. Even a slight mismeasurement can throw your structure out of square.

ASSEMBLING A WALL

Before starting, double-check your plans for overall wall heights and confirm rough openings for windows and doors (page 107).

1 Mark Plates

How fast a wall goes up depends a lot on how much care was taken in marking the plates. The secret to success is to butt the sole and top plates against each other and measure and mark them at the same time. Pros use an X to define a stud, and a T to indicate a trimmer stud.

2 Attach Studs

Once you've measured and cut the wall studs to length, they can be attached to the plates. Position one wall stud at a time and nail it to the top plate. Continue like this until all the framing members have been secured to the top plate, and then repeat the nailing sequence for the sole plate.

3 Square It Up

Before applying sheathing, check the wall for square. Measure diagonally across both sets of opposing corners. If the measurements are the same, the wall is square. To adjust, rack the wall slightly and measure again. When it's square, add a temporary diagonal brace.

4 Add Jack Studs

Cut two jack or trimmer studs to length; typically, these will be 80 inches (standard door height), less the thickness of the sole plate (1½ inches), or 78½ inches. Face-nail one of these to each of the king studs. It's a good idea now to remeasure the width of the opening and the actual width of the door or window to make sure it will fit in the rough opening.

5 Install Headers

The makeup of a header varies according to the distance spanned and the load carried, but most are made of two 2-by members with a ½-inch plywood spacer. Screw or nail the pieces together, position the header, and toenail it to the jack and king studs. Toenail cripple studs between the header and top plate or the sill and sole plate. Add one to each king stud and then space the remaining cripple studs 16 inches on center.

6 Add the Sheathing

For a small structure like a shed, sheathing is most easily installed while the wall is flat. It can be installed horizontally or vertically. Vertical works best for 8-foot-high walls because it can be nailed along all four edges. Install each sheet so the edges are centered on the studs. Attach to the studs with fasteners every 6 inches along the edge and every 12 inches elsewhere. Leave a $\frac{1}{16}$-inch expansion gap between panels.

7 Lift the Wall into Position

With a helper or two, lift the wall up so its top plate is about waist-

high. Keeping the wall tilted slightly forward, slide it toward the edge of the floor until the outside edge aligns with the outside edge of the slab or floor. Raise the wall upright by "walking" your hands down the studs.

8 Brace the Wall

Keep each wall upright until the remaining walls are in place by tacking three 1 × 4 braces to the wall studs, one at each end and one in the middle. Nail the bottom ends into stakes driven into the ground after checking that the wall is plumb. Brace and plumb the remaining walls. If the sheathing has not been applied, measure diagonals inside the structure and adjust for square. Check the walls for level; shim as needed. Fasten the sole plates to the floor or bolt them to a slab. Fasten the corners together and add the double top plates.

9 Attach Vapor Retarder

Add house wrap, building or tar paper, or polyethylene sheeting to limit air movement through walls and prevent heat loss and damage due to moisture. Minimize seams; when they are necessary, provide at least a 12-inch overlap.

10 Add Siding

Once windows and doors are in place (see pages 106–109 for installation instructions), install the clapboard siding. Start by nailing any prefinished inside and outside corner boards. Then snap a level line for the base course and nail a starter strip along the bottom edge of the sheathing to give the siding the proper pitch. Align the starter strip with the chalk line and nail it in place near the top edge. Overlap the next piece and repeat up the wall.

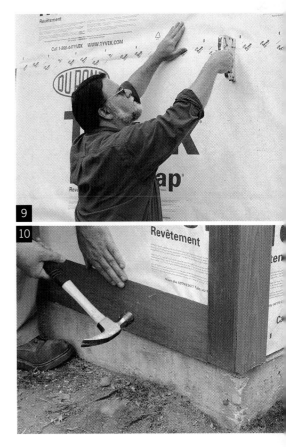

windows and doors

Modern windows have come a long way from the inefficient single-pane units of the past. Now they feature energy-efficient double-insulated panes and tough exteriors.

Doors have evolved as well, with metal exterior doors replacing solid-wood doors. Besides offering better fire protection, metal doors are usually better insulated and won't expand and contract like wood, and their tough exteriors stand up well to constant use and abuse.

WOOD

Solid-wood windows and doors are manufactured using high-grade softwoods (pine) or hardwoods (usually poplar). They are less expensive than clad windows and, if cared for properly, will last decades. One big advantage over clad windows is that wood windows readily accept paint—clad windows don't. If you want a trim color other than the options offered by clad window manufacturers, a solid wood may be the way to go.

CLAD

A clad window features the strength of solid wood, but its exposed surfaces are clad with maintenance-free vinyl or aluminum, usually available in a choice of colors. Screens are often an integral part of the system, so it's unnecessary to install storm window and screen combination units to handle the varying needs of the seasons. Most newer clad windows offer simulated divided lights or grilles, and come in many styles.

VINYL

Solid-vinyl windows offer a number of advantages over solid-wood and clad windows: They're generally cheaper, are readily available as stock items at most home centers in a variety of sizes, and offer maintenance-free interiors and exteriors that don't expand and contract like wood sashes. In addition, they won't chip, peel, or decay over time.

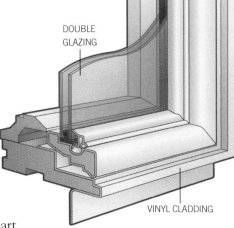

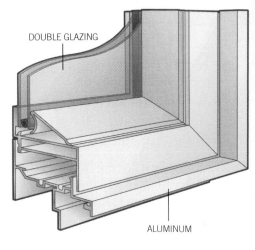

As with the other types of windows, solid-vinyl windows offer grille and screen options.

ALUMINUM

Metal doors and windows have a number of advantages over their wood cousins. First, because they're metal, they won't swell or contract with seasonal changes in humidity as a wood unit does. Second, metal doors and windows are tough—they stand up very well to regular use (and abuse). Metal doors and windows are available in a multitude of shape and sizes; metal doors can even be found covered with a wood veneer to give the appearance of solid wood.

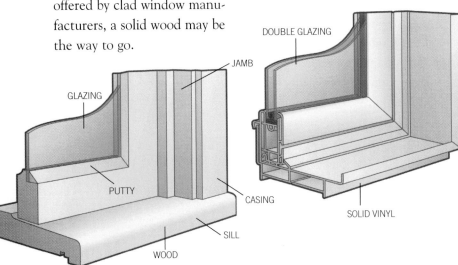

ROUGH OPENINGS

Whenever you need to add a window or door to a wall, you'll need to frame a rough opening. Stud placement is critical here for the window or door to fit properly. In most cases, the rough opening should be ½ inch to ¾ inch wider and taller than the unit you're installing (consult the manufacturer's instruction sheet for the recommended gap). This extra space lets you wedge in shims to adjust the unit for level and plumb. Stick to the recommended gap. Make it too large, and the fasteners you use to secure the unit may penetrate only into the shims and not into the jack or trimmer studs; make it too small, and you either won't be able to fit the unit in or won't have enough play to plumb and level it.

FRAMING FOR A WINDOW The blue arrows in the window shown at right identify the finished opening; the green arrows define the rough opening. The framing members for a window are similar to those of a door: king studs, jack studs, and header. The only difference is the addition of cripple studs beneath the sill plate and above the header (unless the header doesn't completely fill the space above the window as shown). King studs are installed first, followed by jack studs and the header. The opening is completed by adding the cripple studs.

FRAMING FOR A DOOR The blue arrows in the door shown at right identify the finished opening of the door; the green arrows show the rough opening. When framing (see pages 104–105), install the king studs first, the jack or trimmer studs, and then the header. Note that there's a gap at the bottom of the door for the threshold. It may be installed later, or might come as part of the unit if it's a pre-hung door.

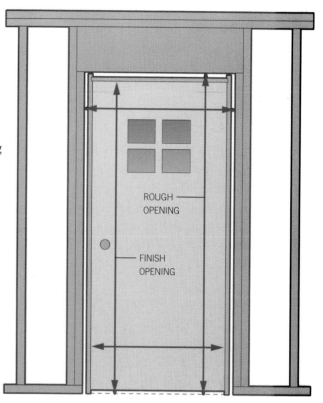

ROUGH OPENING

FINISH OPENING

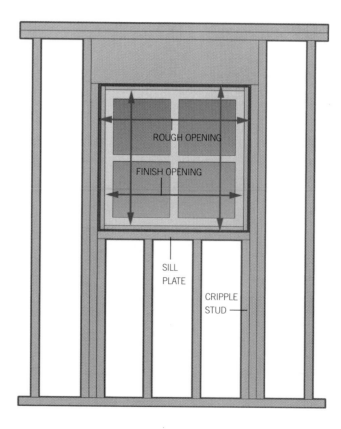

ROUGH OPENING

FINISH OPENING

SILL PLATE

CRIPPLE STUD

INSTALLING A WINDOW OR DOOR

If you've sized the rough opening properly (see page 107), installing a window or door is simple. With a prehung door, the jambs are assembled and the door is hinged to the jamb. On exterior prehung doors, the threshold is typically in place. The tricky part is making sure the unit is level and plumb; check and recheck before securing the unit to the framing.

1 Cut the Opening

Inside of the structure, drive 8d nails through the sheathing at the corners of the rough opening. Run a chalk line around the nails on the exterior and snap a line. Remove nails and drill a ¾-inch access hole in each corner. Use

a reciprocating saw (shown) or saber saw to cut the opening.

2 Apply Moisture Seal

If you're using a vapor retarder like house wrap or building paper, leave enough excess around the window and door openings so that you can wrap it around the framed opening to create a seal. Staple it in place, or use self-adhesive moisture wraps that apply to the framed opening and overlap onto the sheathing.

3 Install Window or Door

Before you position the window or door in the opening, run a bead of exterior-grade caulk around the opening to ensure a tight seal. With the aid of a helper, lift the unit into the opening. Have your helper hold the unit while you go inside to adjust its position.

4 Level and Shim

Slip pairs of shims between the jamb and the framed opening, two pairs on each side, top and bottom. Check for level and plumb, and adjust the shims as necessary. Attach with finishing nails run

through the jamb, shims, and into the frame.

5 Secure to Exterior

For exterior wood trim (often referred to as brick mold), drive 3-inch galvanized casing nails into the framing. With nailing flanges, drive nails through the perforated flange and into the framing.

6 Secure the Jamb

Drive 2½-inch casing nails through the jambs at the shim locations and into the framing. Trim the shims flush with the jamb. Install a drip cap over each door or window to help direct water away from the opening.

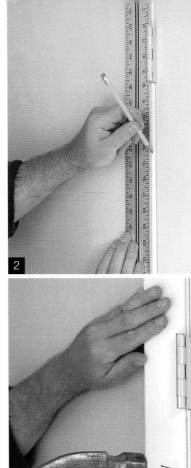

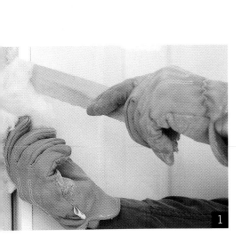

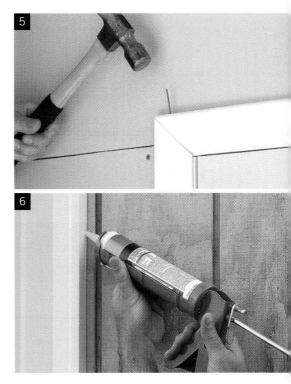

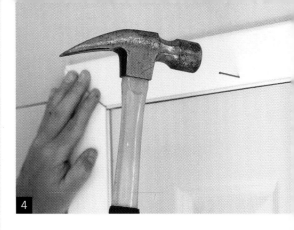

WINDOW AND DOOR TRIM

Install interior window and door trim after wall coverings are in place. For exterior trim, 1 × 4 pine works well—attach it with galvanized casing nails driven into the framing.

1 Insulate Around the Window

If you're planning to insulate your building, take the time before you attach the interior trim to stuff some fiberglass insulation in any gaps between the window or door jamb and the framing. This will help reduce drafts and heat loss.

2 Mark the Reveal

Before installing the interior trim for a door or window, draw a set-back line or "reveal" ¼ inch in from the inside of the jamb. Align each of the side trim pieces with this line and mark them where they intersect the top reveal line.

3 Add the Side Trim

Miter-cut the tops of the side casings with a power miter saw or a hand saw and a miter box. Secure side and top trim to the jamb with 2-inch finishing nails, aligning the inside edges with the reveal lines.

Drive 2½-inch casing nails through the outer edge of the trim and into the framing.

4 Install Top Trim

Whenever you attach trim with nails, stop hammering when the head of the nail is about ¼ inch away from the surface. This prevents nasty dings in the trim, which would have to be sanded out or filled with putty. Drive the protruding nail the rest of the way in using a nail set. Set the nails about ⅛ inch below the surface, fill with putty, and sand flush when dry.

5 Lock-nail Corners

To prevent the mitered corners of the trim from opening up over time and creating a gap, drive a 2-inch finishing nail through the top trim about 1 inch from the end and into the side trim. To keep the mitered pieces from splitting, drill a ¹⁄₁₆-inch pilot hole through the trim pieces before nailing.

6 Seal with Caulk

Complete your window or door trim by running a bead of silicone caulk around the exterior trim to create a watertight seal. If there are any gaps between the interior trim and the wall covering, run a bead of paintable latex caulk around the trim to fill them.

roofing

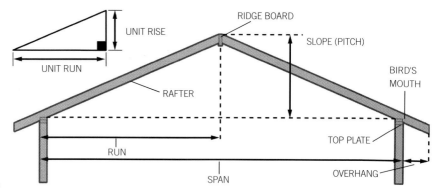

Most shed, garage, and barn roofs are variations on the simple gable roof. In a gable roof, evenly spaced pairs of rafters run from the top plates of the wall up to the ridge board (see drawing at right). A roof overhang often extends past the walls. The ends of the rafters are usually covered with trim called the fascia.

Roof framing begins by installing ceiling joists, then the rafters and ridge board, and, if required, collar ties. (Collar ties attach horizontally to rafters below the peak to keep rafters from spreading apart.) Depending on the size of your structure, rafters can be 2 × 4s for a small shed, or up to 2 × 10s or larger for garages and barns. They're usually spaced at 16-inch or 24-inch centers. (Check with your building department for rafter dimension and spacing required by local codes.) The length of the rafter will depend on the slope of the roof (see chart below). With the length determined, measure and mark, and cut one rafter and use it as a pattern to make the rest. The slope or pitch of a roof is defined as a rafter's vertical rise in inches (or unit rise) per 12 inches of horizontal run (see the drawing). For example, a rafter that rises 5 inches for every 12 inches of run has a 5:12 or 5-in-12 slope. Roofs with steeper slopes require longer rafters and are better able to shed snow (use a minimum of 6 in 12 for snowy areas). Roofs with lower slopes work fine in warmer climates—generally a minimum of at least 3 in 12.

DETERMINING GABLE RAFTER LENGTH

For runs other than those shown below, use the rafter table imprinted on a framing square. Here's how to use it. If your slope is 8 in 12 (8 inches rise for every 12 inches run) and your run is 16 feet, find the number imprinted below the 8-inch mark—14.42 (14.42 inches per foot of run). Multiply 14.42 by 16 (the run) and you'll get 230.72 inches. Divide by 12 for a rafter length of 19.22 feet. To convert .22 feet to inches, multiply by 12—2.72 inches. To convert .72 to 16ths of an inch, multiply by 16. You'll come up with 11.52 16ths. Total rafter length would be just a tad longer than 19 feet $^{11}/_{16}$ inches.

INCH MARK	2"	3"	4"	5"	6"	7"	8"	9"	10"
Slope	2 in 12	3 in 12	4 in 12	5 in 12	6 in 12	7 in 12	8 in 12	9 in 12	10 in 12
Length per foot run	12.17"	12.37"	12.65"	13"	13.42"	13.89"	14.42"	15"	15.62"
Length per 6' run	73.02"	74.22"	75.9"	78"	80.52"	83.34"	86.52"	90"	93.72"
Length for 12' run	146.04"	148.44"	151.8"	156"	161.04"	166.68"	173.04"	180"	187.44"
INCH MARK	11"	12"	13"	14"	15"	16"	17"	18"	
Slope	11 in 12	12 in 12	13 in 12	14 in 12	15 in 12	16 in 12	17 in 12	18 in 12	
Length per foot run	16.28"	16.97"	17.69"	18.44"	19.21"	20"	20.81"	21.63"	
Length per 6' run	97.68"	101.82"	106.14"	110.64"	115.26"	120"	124.86"	129.78"	
Length for 12' run	195.36"	203.64"	212.28"	221.28"	230.52"	240"	249.72"	259.56"	

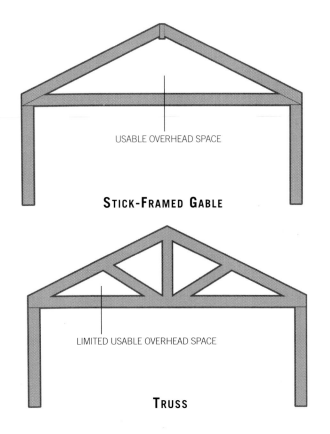

USABLE OVERHEAD SPACE

STICK-FRAMED GABLE

LIMITED USABLE OVERHEAD SPACE

TRUSS

TRUSSES

As structures get larger, the framing members of conventional stick-framed roofs must get beefier to handle the larger span. An alternative to this is to use a prefabricated truss designed to support a roof over a wide span. A suitably designed truss eliminates the need for load-bearing partitions below and greatly simplifies framing so the roof can be put up quickly. (Engineered trusses can be ordered through most full-service lumberyards—just provide them with the building size and the desired roof pitch.) One major disadvantage to roof trusses is the loss of attic space.

All trusses consist of three main parts: upper chords serving as rafters, lower chords acting as ceiling joists, and web members that tie the chords together. The parts of the truss are typically held together with metal or wood gusset plates. The king post truss is a simple truss system that can span only distances less than 25 feet. Fink trusses are the most common and can span over 40 feet. A scissors truss can also span 40 feet and allows for slightly more interior space.

Trusses are generally installed by first placing them upside down on the top plates and then flipping them up into position one at a time. It's easiest if you start at one end of the structure and attach 2 × 4 braces to the gable ends to support the first truss. (Another option is to run long 2 × 4 braces from the brace to the ground and secure them at the bottom to stakes driven firmly into the ground.)

Have workers on ladders at each end holding the truss in position while another worker in the middle pushes the truss up with a long pole. Toenail the ends of the truss and temporarily fasten the top to the 2 × 4 braces on the gable end. As more trusses are added, use 1 × 4 bracing to temporarily attach them to the previous truss so they'll keep in alignment until the roof sheathing can be applied.

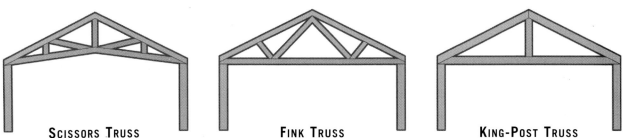

SCISSORS TRUSS **FINK TRUSS** **KING-POST TRUSS**

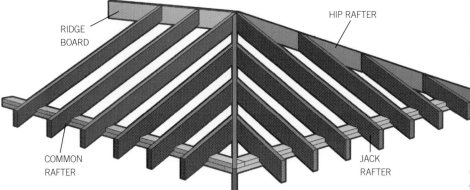

RIDGE BOARD

HIP RAFTER

COMMON RAFTER

JACK RAFTER

HIP FRAMING

Because of the multiple angled cuts required for the rafters that run between the ridge board and the top plates (see drawing above), a hip roof is one of the more complicated options for roof framing. Adding to the confusion are the specialized names of many of the parts. Common rafters (blue in the drawing) run the full distance from the ridge (yellow in drawing) to the double top plates. Hip rafters (green in drawing) connect to the ridge at an angle where the two planes of the roof meet. The jack rafters (red in drawing) run from the hip rafter to the eaves.

CEILING JOISTS

Ceiling joists are horizontal framing members that span the top plates of the structure and prevent the roof load from bowing the walls apart. Ceiling joists for large structures often rest on a beam or load-bearing wall at the midpoint. Like rafters, the size of joists will depend on the size of the structure. As a general rule, the larger the structure, the beefier the joists. Typical spacing is 16-inch or 24-inch on center.

If you're planning to use the ceiling joists to support a floor above, you'll want to go with 16-inch spacing. Here again, you should check your local building code for requirements. On some structures, the ceiling joists are replaced with collar ties. This creates more headroom but doesn't allow space for overhead storage. Depending on how the rafters are attached to the top plates, you may or may not need to trim the end to match the rafter (right).

EAVES AND SOFFITS

When the bottoms of rafters extend out past the walls of a structure, the overhang they form is called the eaves. A soffit (also called a cornice) is the underside of the rafters at the eaves. This area may be left open, or the ends of the rafters can be covered with trim called fascia (see drawings at right). The soffit area may also be closed in as long as care is taken to provide vents to allow

air to circulate. Some soffit materials such as vinyl and aluminum soffit panels have special perforated panels that are placed every 10 feet or so. Other venting options include round, rectangular, or continuous metal vents. The round variety are easiest to install—all you need to do is drill a hole in the soffit material and snap the vent in place.

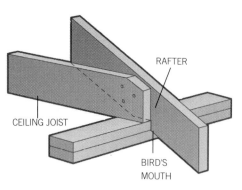

RAFTER

CEILING JOIST

BIRD'S MOUTH

RAFTERS AND CEILING JOISTS

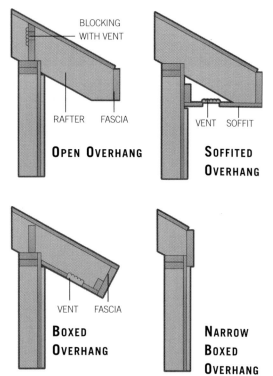

BLOCKING WITH VENT

RAFTER   FASCIA

OPEN OVERHANG

VENT   SOFFIT

SOFFITED OVERHANG

VENT   FASCIA

BOXED OVERHANG

NARROW BOXED OVERHANG

ROOFING MATERIALS

Roofing materials vary widely in appearance, durability, and ease of installation. Sheds and garages lend themselves to asphalt or wood shingles, while larger structures often use metal roofing. Regardless of the material used, all these structures need flashing to protect and seal the roof.

FLASHING Protect exposed materials and seal seams and openings by adding flashing to your structure. It can be made of galvanized sheet metal, aluminum, copper, and sometimes rubber or plastic. Metal flashing is available in rolls that you can cut and bend yourself. Typical flashing includes drip edge to cover the ends of eaves and rakes; vent collars, which seal the openings around vents; Z-flashing, which seals above windows and doors; and step flashing used along walls, dormers, and chimneys. To secure the flashing, use fasteners made of the same material as the flashing. This prevents a chemical reaction that can produce corrosion.

SHINGLES Asphalt-based shingles are the most common roofing material, as they are inexpensive, easy to install, and last 15 to 20 years. They are available in a wide variety of colors and styles, the most popular styles being architectural, random tab, and three-tab strips. They are suitable for every

STEP FLASHING

GALVANIZED SHEET METAL

DRIP EDGE

DRIP EDGE

RUBBER VENT COLLAR

ALUMINUM

ALUMINUM VENT COLLAR

COPPER

WOOD SHAKES

WOOD SHINGLES

ASPHALT SHINGLES

climate but should be used only on roofs with minimum 4-in-12 slope. Wood shingles and shakes weigh less than asphalt shingles and better withstand the freeze/thaw cycles common in cold climates. On the down side, they're expensive and time-consuming to install.

METAL ROOFING Corrugated and standing-seam metal roofing are excellent choices for larger buildings such as barns. In the past, these roofing materials were installed only by pros and were quite expensive. Today, there are economical systems designed for the average homeowner that

snap together. Some metal roofing is coated with baked-on enamel or even vinyl. Because metal roofing expands and contracts with heat and cold, flexible fasteners must be used to keep the fastener holes sealed.

STANDING SEAM

CORRUGATED

FRAMING THE ROOF

Three cuts are needed to make a rafter: a plumb cut where the rafter meets the ridge board, a plumb cut at the eaves end, and a bird's mouth to allow the rafter to fit onto the top plate of the wall. Expect some trial and error.

1 Mark the Plumb Cuts

One way to mark the plumb cuts on a rafter is to hold it against the ridge board, temporarily held in place with vertical supports, and mark the angle. Or, mark the plumb cuts with a framing square. Position the framing square on the rafter so the blade and tongue measurement marks align with the rafter edges to coincide with the rise and run of the roof.

2 Test the Fit

Once you've cut a rafter to length and made the bird's-mouth cut (see box below), use this as a template to make another rafter. Then position these against the ridge board and check to make sure the ends come flush against it while the bird's mouth rests flat on the top plates.

3 Mass-Produce the Rafters

Make your best rafter into a jig by tacking scraps of wood along one edge. Use it to quickly and accurately mark the other rafters. For greatest efficiency, make all the circular saw cuts first, then finish the bird's mouth with a hand saw.

CUTTING A BIRD'S MOUTH

It's easiest to lay out a bird's-mouth cut by having a helper hold a rafter against the ridge board. Then hold the tail end against the top plate and draw around the top plate to locate the notch in the rafter.

Next, set the blade of a circular saw for maximum depth and make the bird's-mouth cuts. Stop the cuts where the lines intersect. This won't cut out the notch completely; cutting past the marks will weaken the rafter.

Finally, use a hand saw to complete the cuts to remove the waste. If necessary, use a sharp chisel to clean up any rough edges, especially in the corner so that the notch will rest flat on the top plates.

ADDING SHEATHING AND ASPHALT SHINGLES

If you're planning on asphalt roofing, you'll need to install plywood sheathing. (Metal roofing doesn't require sheathing, and wood shingles use 1 × 4s spaced to expose the desired amount of shingle.) The most critical part of installing shingles is the starter course. This course is installed with the tabs up instead of down to position the adhesive so it will adhere the first row to the roof. It must be installed exactly straight.

1 Install the Sheathing

Apply plywood sheathing on the roof framing by beginning in the bottom corner of one side. Place the long side perpendicular to the rafters so the opposite edge is centered on a rafter. Secure the sheathing with 8d galvanized nails every 6 inches along the edges and every 12 inches elsewhere.

Use panel clips to support the edges of plywood sheathing between rafters. The U-shaped clips snap onto the edges of adjoining sheathing. Stagger the

ends of the sheathing to keep the seams from aligning and weakening the roof. Start the second piece with a half sheet, and then stagger every other panel.

2 Add Roofing Felt

Once the sheathing is in place, add the drip edge and roofing felt. Nail on a metal drip edge along the eaves and the rake. Then roll out roofing felt and staple it every 10 or 12 inches. Overlap horizontal seams 2 inches and vertical seams 12 inches.

3 Add Starter Row

Because all of the shingles will use the starter row as a reference, it's important to make sure it goes down straight. Start by snapping a chalk line on the felt to define the top of the starter course. Secure each shingle with a galvanized roofing nail above each notch.

4 Add Remaining Courses

The first and remaining courses are all installed with the tabs pointing down. Nail each shingle to the roof just above the slot between the tabs. Start the second course with an offset of about 6 inches to stagger the seams.

5 Trim the Ends

To save time, let the shingles overhang the edges or "run wild." Then come back once the side of the roof is complete and trim them all at once. You can do this with a sharp utility knife or a pair of heavy-duty shears.

finishing touches

Once there's a roof on your structure and the exterior is closed in, you can turn to finishing the interior. This may include adding electrical circuits (see below), plumbing (page 118), insulation and heat (pages 119–120), and covering the interior walls (pages 121–122). You may want to turn your space into a specialty area such as a workshop or craft space (page 123) and add storage (page 124) and a ramp or stairs (page 125).

ADDING POWER

Any shed, garage, or barn you build will be more functional if you run power to it. You'll be able to light up the interior at night, use power tools and appliances—even install heating and cooling. Getting the power there is the tough part; interior wiring is straightforward and can be added by the average homeowner,

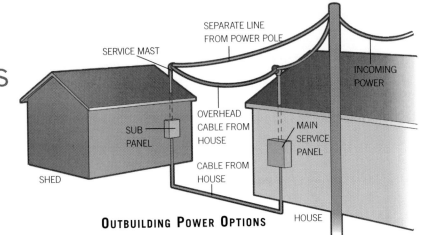

OUTBUILDING POWER OPTIONS

though some local codes require that all or part of the wiring be done by a pro.

POWER OPTIONS One way to route power to a structure is to run buried wires (marked red, above) from your home's service panel to the structure. To do this, you must have sufficient capacity available at the service panel. (If in doubt, check with a licensed electrician.) You may have to upgrade the panel—an expensive proposition. With the power source established, you can dig a trench (check local codes for the required depth) and bury UF (underground feeder) cable.

Or, encase separate wires in metal or plastic conduit.

Another approach is to run a power line overhead from the nearest power pole (marked in blue) or from the house (green). Any overhead lines should be installed by an electrician.

TYPICAL SYSTEM Depending on your power needs, you can run a single 20-amp cable that ends in a standard junction box, a 40- to 60-amp cable feeding a subpanel, or up to a 100-amp line that powers a service panel. From the service panel, subpanel, or junction box, the wiring branches out into circuits—a single branch for an

TYPICAL OUTBUILDING ELECTRICAL SYSTEM

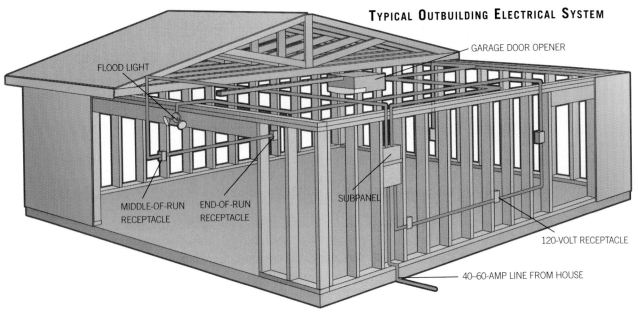

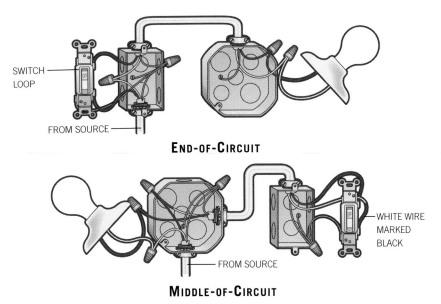

SWITCH LOOP

FROM SOURCE

END-OF-CIRCUIT

FROM SOURCE

WHITE WIRE MARKED BLACK

MIDDLE-OF-CIRCUIT

overhead light and a couple of receptacles, or multiple branches.

Because local codes supersede national codes, check with your local building department for material and installation specifications. Electrical code specifies everything from how high a receptacle is mounted to the number of wires allowed in a junction box. Nonmetallic cable (NM) makes wiring simple since no conduit is required. All you do to route the cable through ceilings and walls is to drill access holes for the cable.

Making the final connection from the power source to a sub-

panel or service panel is best done by a licensed electrician. Make sure to have the wiring inspected before wall coverings are added, or you'll have to remove them for inspection.

WIRING LIGHTS How you wire an overhead light will depend on whether the light fixture is at the end of a circuit run or in the middle (see above). Incoming power may run to the switch box first and then on to one or more light fixtures. Or, the power can come into the light fixture box and the switch loop is connected to route power through the

switch. In a switch loop, the two-conductor cable has one white and one black wire. In some cases, the white wire may be used to carry current; in such situations, you must identify the white wire as hot by wrapping it with black electrician's tape.

WIRING RECEPTACLES As with lighting fixtures, how you wire a receptacle will depend on whether it's in the middle or at the end of a run. In most cases, a series of receptacles are run in parallel. All grounded receptacles have color-coded terminals. The brass-colored terminals are hot and connect to the black wires. The silver-colored terminals are neutral and connect to white wires. The green-colored terminal is ground and connects to a green-colored wire or an uninsulated copper wire. Use ground-fault circuit interrupter (GFCI) receptacles near sinks or in damp areas (check local codes). Every receptacle must be grounded. Metal boxes (shown below) must be grounded as well.

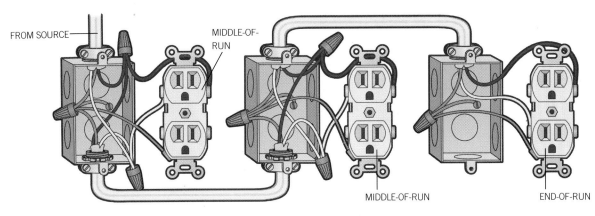

FROM SOURCE

MIDDLE-OF-RUN

MIDDLE-OF-RUN

END-OF-RUN

WIRING RECEPTACLES

RUNNING PLUMBING

Although most people would prefer to have running water in a shed, garage, or barn, it may not be feasible. Much will depend on your budget and, especially, your local climate—it will define your options for running water and waste lines to the new structure.

PLUMBING OPTIONS In warm climates, you can get by with burying a garden hose a few inches below the lawn, then making a simple drain pit to serve as the septic or sewer (see the drawing above right). In colder climates, the water and waste lines need to be installed well below the frost line—in some areas as much as 4 to 5 feet deep. What's more, tapping into existing lines—particularly waste lines—is a job best left to a licensed plumber. How deep the lines must be buried, the type of materials you use, and even

who can make the connections, will be defined by local code.

TYPICAL SYSTEM In a typical outbuilding, a single cold-water line is run from the house. Likewise, a waste line runs out to the building, but slopes down back toward the house so it will drain. At the new structure, the waste line terminates in a sanitary tee with a cleanout port. Piping connects to the top of the sanitary tee and continues up and through the roof for venting. The vent allows outside air to replace air displaced by draining water. Without the vent, drains can be sluggish and negative pressure might suck the water out of traps, allowing in sewer gas. Another sanitary tee connects to the sink via a trap. Here again, the piping

PLUMBING OPTIONS

VENT

DRAIN

SUPPLY

FLEXIBLE SUPPLY PROTECTED BY PRESSURE-TREATED PLANK

DRAIN PIT

must slope down toward the tee to allow drainage. The water supply line is terminated in a shutoff valve, which controls water flow to the sink faucet. If you want hot water, don't try to run an insulated line—install a water heater in the outbuilding instead.

TYPICAL OUTBUILDING PLUMBING SYSTEM

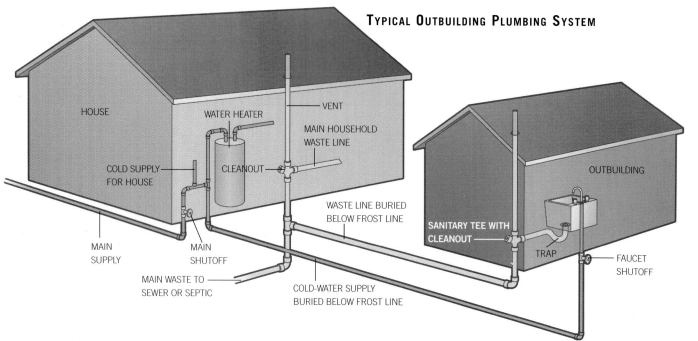

HOUSE

WATER HEATER

VENT

MAIN HOUSEHOLD WASTE LINE

COLD SUPPLY FOR HOUSE

CLEANOUT

OUTBUILDING

MAIN SUPPLY

MAIN SHUTOFF

WASTE LINE BURIED BELOW FROST LINE

SANITARY TEE WITH CLEANOUT

TRAP

FAUCET SHUTOFF

MAIN WASTE TO SEWER OR SEPTIC

COLD-WATER SUPPLY BURIED BELOW FROST LINE

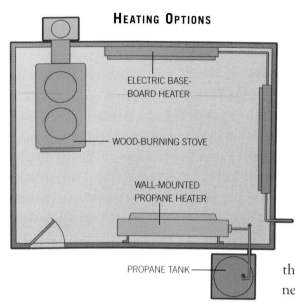

HEATING OPTIONS

ELECTRIC BASE-BOARD HEATER

WOOD-BURNING STOVE

WALL-MOUNTED PROPANE HEATER

PROPANE TANK

HEATING YOUR BUILDING

If you need to heat your new building, there are a number of economical alternatives to installing a furnace. Where local codes permit, small and medium structures can be effectively heated with a wood stove, electric heater, or propane heater.

WOOD-BURNING STOVE Sealed wood-burning stoves can be quite efficient and are easy to install. Local codes will specify if you can use wood heat or not, how far away from the wall the stove must be installed, and the type of noncombustible wall covering that must be mounted near the stove. Chimney kits are available that virtually snap together. All you do is cut a hole in the side of your building at the appropriate height and install a bracket or two on the exterior to support the stack. The downside to wood heat is the difficulty of maintaining an even temperature while keeping the stove stoked with wood.

ELECTRIC HEAT If electrical service is available, electric baseboard heat is clean and quick to install. On the minus side, most baseboards require 220 volts to operate, and heating with electricity can be expensive.

PROPANE HEAT Another option that works well if local code allows is heating with propane. There are a number of wall-mounted units available that are capable of easily heating a two- to three-car garage. Some models are manually controlled, while others come with thermostats. With propane heat, you'll need to have a tank and a gas line installed to the heater. Most propane companies provide the tank for free and will maintain and fill the tank as required.

PLANNING FOR INSULATION

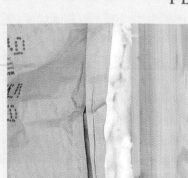

The variety of material options (see page 120) make walls easy to insulate. Choices include fiberglass batts, rigid foam, and blown-in insulation. Fiberglass is the most popular, as it's inexpensive and quick to install.

How you insulate a ceiling will depend on whether or not the space above will be used. If it will be used, you can add fiberglass between the joists or blow in cellulose. For spaces that won't be used, lay down thick batts of insulation for the ultimate in energy efficiency.

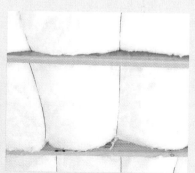

Floors present an insulating challenge since there's nothing under the floor joists to support the insulation. Fiberglass insulation is typically installed between the joists and held up with wire supports or chicken wire.

FIBERGLASS BATTS

FACED FIBERGLASS

RIGID FOAM

CELLULOSE

INSULATING MATERIALS

Fiberglass insulation is inexpensive and offers R-values ranging from R-11 to R-35, depending on thickness. It's available in a variety of widths (designed to fit between 16-inch- and 24-inch-spaced studs and joists) and backings. You can purchase rolls or precut lengths designed to fit in the standard wall. Unfaced insulation is press-fit between studs and joists without the use of fasteners. Faced insulation is pressed in place and then stapled. Fiberglass can irritate the skin, eyes, and lungs, so wear long pants, a long-sleeved shirt, gloves, goggles, and a dust mask.

Extruded polystyrene (or rigid foam) insulation is a dense foam board that generally offers around R-5 per inch of thickness. It's inexpensive and comes in 4 × 8-foot sheets or strips designed to fit between 16- or 24-inch-on-center studs or joists. Sheets usually have tongue-and-groove edges so they can be joined together to create a continuous layer of insulation. Rigid foam can be press-fit in place or secured with construction adhesive or nails and screws.

Cellulose loose fill is commonly made from recycled paper combined with a flame retardant. Its R-value is similar to that of fiberglass—about R-3.5 per inch of thickness. Loose fill can be blown in and is an excellent choice for ceilings with low clearances where installing fiberglass would be difficult. However, it settles with age.

INSTALLING FIBERGLASS
Measure from top to bottom, add 3 inches, and cut a strip of insulation to length. Press the strip between the framing and overlap the facing onto the framing. Begin stapling at the top and work your way down both sides, finishing with the bottom.

ADDING FOAM
Precut strips of rigid foam make installation a snap. Measure between top and bottom and cut the strip to match with a utility knife or a hand saw. If desired, apply a bead of construction adhesive around the perimeter of the foam and press the foam into place.

USING INSULATION SUPPORTS
Fiberglass can be installed in ceilings with the aid of insulation supports. These are lengths of heavy-gauge wire with chisel-tip ends. Press one end of the support into the ceiling joist and then flex it to fit the other end into the opposing joist. If the insulation is faced, it's a good idea to add a few staples to keep the insulation from shifting over time.

ADHERING RIGID FOAM
Foam insulation is the perfect choice for angled ceilings. Precut strips make this job easier, since all you need to do is cut them to length. Apply a generous bead of construction adhesive around the perimeter and an "X" from top to bottom, and press the strip in place.

Labels in top image: HARDBOARD, DRYWALL, PERFORATED HARDBOARD, T1-11, PANELING, PLYWOOD

INTERIOR WALLS

Interior walls can be left bare or covered. If you've added insulation, it's best to cover the walls to prevent damage to the insulation over time. Whatever material you decide on, make sure to have all inspections completed before closing in the walls.

MATERIAL OPTIONS Drywall is an economical and easy-to-install wall covering; ½-inch will hold up better than thinner varieties. (See page 122 for step-by-step installation instructions.)

Another excellent option for covering interior walls is T1-11 siding. Although more expensive than drywall, T1-11 siding can handle the day-to-day abuse the interior walls of an outbuilding get without showing any dings or dents. Plus, since its minimum thickness is an ample ½ inch and it's plywood, you can hang tools, cabinets, almost anything to it without using wall anchors.

If you're planning on using your new building as living space, consider wood paneling. It's available in many colors and patterns and goes up quickly with construction adhesive and matching nails. For workspace, plain hardboard and plywood are hardworking, low-cost options.

FASTENERS Drywall is attached with either nails or screws. T1-11, hardboard, and plywood are best secured with trim-head screws, as their smaller heads are less noticeable. Paneling is usually fastened with construction adhesive and held in place with color-matched nails.

Labels: CONSTRUCTION ADHESIVE, DRYWALL SCREWS, DRYWALL NAILS, TRIM-HEAD SCREWS, PANEL NAILS

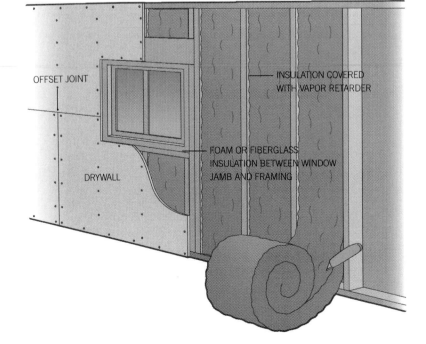

Labels: OFFSET JOINT, INSULATION COVERED WITH VAPOR RETARDER, FOAM OR FIBERGLASS INSULATION BETWEEN WINDOW JAMB AND FRAMING, DRYWALL

FINISHING AN INTERIOR WALL

Finishing off an interior wall usually begins by installing insulation and vapor retarder. Then the wall covering is added and is attached to the wall studs. Wall coverings around windows and doors should butt firmly up against the window or door jamb. Any gaps should be filled with foam insulation or scraps of fiberglass to prevent drafts before trim is added (see page 109 for directions on installing trim).

INSTALLING DRYWALL

To cut drywall, draw a line with a straightedge (a drywall T-square is ideal), and cut along this line with a sharp utility knife. Flip the sheet over and lift up one end to snap the sheet. Run your utility knife along the inside crease to cut completely through the sheet.

1 Center on Studs

Position the first sheet of drywall tight in a corner so the opposite end is centered on a wall stud. Install the sheets horizontally to make taping faster and easier. If the opposite end of the sheet isn't centered on the studs, remove and trim it. Offset the sheets so taped joints won't be obvious.

2 Secure the Sheet

Drywall nails go in faster, but they have a tendency to "pop" over time as the studs dry out. If you're using screws, drive them in so they sit just below the surface, but don't break the paper covering.

3 Apply Tape

To conceal the joints between the sheets of drywall, apply drywall tape over the gaps. Tape may be self-adhesive or nonstick. With self-adhesive tape, just press it into place; to apply nonadhesive tape, first spread on a thin coat of joint compound and then press the tape into the compound with a wide-blade putty knife.

4 Apply Joint Compound

Apply a first coat of joint compound over the tape and the "dimples" left by the screws, with a 4- to 6-inch-wide drywall knife. Work it as smooth as possible—don't depend on sanding to remove anything but minor imperfections.

5 Feather and Smooth

When the first coat has dried, apply a second coat with a wider drywall knife. Work the compound gently away from the joint to "feather" it for a smooth transition. You may have to feather in stages, allowing the compound to dry between each coat. Give the walls a light sanding with a pole sander (a tool with a sanding pad attached to a pole) to knock off imperfections. When the joint compound is dry, the final step is to smooth the surface to remove any remaining imperfections. Use a slightly damp drywall sponge and rub with a swirling motion to smooth and level the surface.

SPECIALTY AREAS

Added storage space isn't the only reason people build sheds, barns, and garages; many want a place to pursue a hobby. Two common activities centers are an area for crafts and a workshop for woodworking or all-purpose tinkering.

CRAFTS AREA A sturdy table or two and some storage space are the essentials for a crafts area. The simple table shown at right consists of a top and bottom 2-by frame and a top, shelf, and legs made of plywood. Plastic laminate can be attached to the top with contact cement to create a tough surface that won't stain.

A great way to organize your craft supplies is to build a wall-mounted organizer like the one shown in the drawing. It's nothing more than a piece of ¼-inch peg-

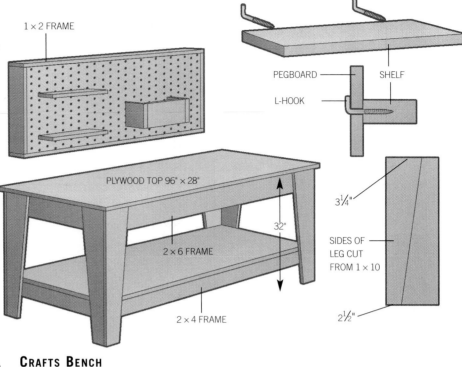

1 × 2 FRAME

PEGBOARD   SHELF

L-HOOK

PLYWOOD TOP 96" × 28"

2 × 6 FRAME

32"

2 × 4 FRAME

3¼"

SIDES OF LEG CUT FROM 1 × 10

2½"

CRAFTS BENCH

board set into a 1 × 4 frame. The pegboard accepts standard peg hooks or shop-made shelves and containers that use L-hooks as hangers.

WORKSHOP With a little ingenuity and some mobile bases, you can shoehorn a workshop into almost any garage. If space allows, you might be able to take up one half of a two-car garage (as shown below left). If you don't have this luxury, consider placing your tools on wheels—mobile bases are available for almost any tool. Or, you can make your own with a set of locking casters and a layer or two of ¾-inch-thick plywood. When not in use, the tools can be rolled up against the walls or back into a corner. You can even put a workbench on wheels if necessary. A workshop needs plenty of power for both tools and lighting—be sure to allow for this in your plans.

PLANNING FOR A GARAGE WORKSHOP

LUMBER RACK

DRILL PRESS

TABLE SAW

WORKBENCH

BAND SAW

JOINTER

SCRAP BIN

SHELVING

PLANNING FOR STORAGE

No matter how large or small your new shed, garage, or barn, you'll want to maximize the storage space inside. Here are storage ideas you can adapt to meet the needs of your new structure.

ORGANIZER SYSTEM A modular organizer system, like the one above right, features a work surface and shelves that can be raised and lowered as needed. Cut cleats from 2-by stock. Drill ¾-inch holes in the cleats every 4 inches for dowels that will hold the shelf brackets. Attach the cleats vertically to wall studs with lag bolts. Each shelf bracket has a 2-by core sandwiched between a pair of ¼-inch-thick hardboard sides with ¾-inch holes for the dowel pins that hold the bracket to the cleat. When assembling the brackets, make sure the top edges are flush and the holes in the outer sides align. Cut ¾-inch dowels into 2¼-inch lengths—you'll need one for every bracket. Once brackets are in place, cut shelves from ¾-inch solid pine or plywood. Secure each shelf to the bracket by driving screws in through the top of the shelf.

OTHER STORAGE IDEAS Make the most of the space where ceiling meets walls by hanging shelves on suspended 2-by hangers. Cleats affixed perpendicular to the hanger bottoms attach to the studs to support the shelving.

Simple shelves can be made by notching scraps of 2 × 6 or 2 × 8 to fit around wall studs and screwing them in place.

It's easy to construct 1 × 4 shelving by first gluing and screwing short cleats to the wall studs. Then you cut shelves to fit between the studs and screw them to the cleats.

In a garage, create storage space above parked cars by building a platform made from a 2 × 4 frame covered with plywood.

CLEAT 1½" × 2"
1-BY SHELF
20"
DESK SHELF BRACKET
SCREW SECURES SHELF
2-BY CORE
¾" × 2" DOWEL
¼" HARDBOARD
10"
ATTACH CLEATS TO WALL STUDS WITH LAG SCREWS

WALL ORGANIZER

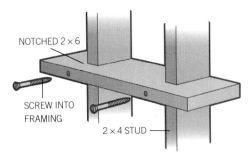

2 × 2 HANGER
2 × 2 CLEAT
¾" PLYWOOD

UNDER-RAFTER SHELVING

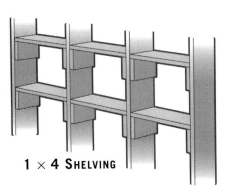

NOTCHED 2 × 6
SCREW INTO FRAMING
2 × 4 STUD

2 × 6 SHELVING

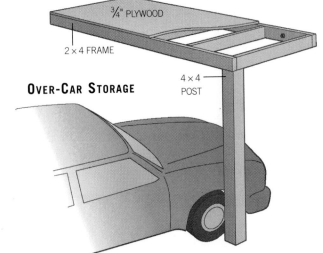

¾" PLYWOOD
2 × 4 FRAME
4 × 4 POST

OVER-CAR STORAGE

1 × 4 SHELVING

ADDING STAIRS AND RAMPS

Stairs or a ramp must attach securely to your shed, garage, or barn with joist hangers or a ledger, and to a concrete footing at ground level. Most building codes allow for a shallow footing installed over pea gravel for drainage; check with your local building department. When you chat with the building department folks, ask whether handrails are required for your stairs or ramp.

STAIRS Typical shed stairs consist of two or three stringers and treads (see the drawing above right). Although you can purchase precut stringers, odds are that they won't fit your building. To make your own, first establish the rise and run of the steps. Total rise is the distance from the ground to the floor of the structure; unit rise is the height of each step. Total run (how far the steps will extend out) requires some math.

Start by dividing the total rise by 7 inches (the recommended unit rise or height of each step) to find out how many steps you'll need (round off to the nearest whole number).

To calculate total run, multiply the unit run (or stair width) by the number of treads (always 1 less than the number of steps). If you're using two 2 × 6s for the treads, the unit run will be 10 inches (this allows for a gap between them and a slight over-

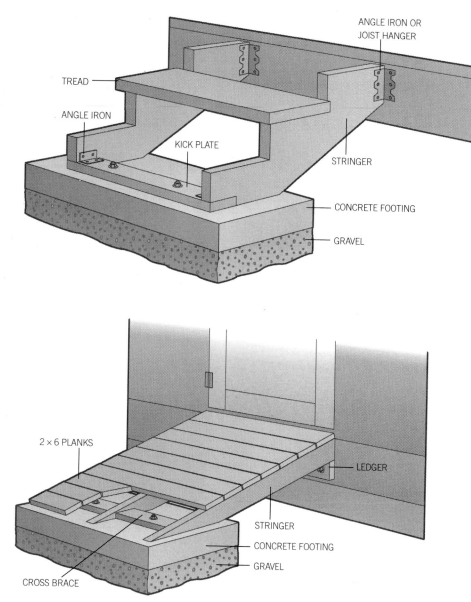

hang). For example, a total rise of 40 inches divided by 7 inches equals 5.7; rounding up gives 6 steps (5 treads). So total run is 10 inches times 5, or 50 inches. To find your actual unit rise, divide your measured total rise by the number of steps. In this example, actual unit rise equals 40 inches divided by 6, roughly 6⅝ inches.

RAMP A ramp is a lot easier to build than stairs because no treads are involved. All you need to do is decide on the slope for the ramp and cut the ends of the stringers accordingly. The slope is measured in inches of vertical rise per linear foot. A 1-in-8 slope will do for most utility work; for wheelchair access, use a 1-in-12 slope.

glossary

ANCHOR BOLT A bolt, usually J-shaped, that is set into freshly cast concrete with the threaded end projecting above the surface.

BACKFILL Soil or gravel used to fill between a foundation and the ground excavated around it.

BATTEN A strip of lumber used to seal vertical siding; a base for fastening some types of roofing.

BATTERBOARD Staked horizontal board that supports string used to lay out a foundation.

BEARING WALL A wall that supports joists at their ends or midspan, transferring weight to the girder, columns, or foundation wall. All exterior walls, as well as some interior walls, are bearing.

BIRD'S MOUTH A notch cut near the end of a rafter to fit over a double top plate.

BLOCKING Pieces of wood installed between joists or studs to give rigidity to the structure or to provide a nailing surface.

BRIDGING Steel braces or wood blocks that are installed in an X pattern between floor joists to stabilize the joists.

CDX An economical, low-grade exterior plywood sheathing.

CHORDS Framing members that make up the two sides of the roof and the base of a triangular truss.

CODES Regulations implemented by your local building department that control the design and construction of structures.

COLLAR TIE A horizontal framing member installed between rafters to add stiffness.

CORNICE The part of the roof that overhangs a wall; also called the roof overhang.

CRIPPLE STUDS Short vertical studs installed between a header and a top plate or between a rough sill and the sole plate.

CURING The process by which concrete/mortar hardens; it requires keeping the surface moist for several days.

DIMENSION LUMBER Lumber intended for structural framing and graded for strength. From 2 inches to 4 inches thick and at least 2 inches wide.

DOUBLE TOP PLATE Typically 2-by material attached to the top plate of a structure to tie walls together.

DRIP EDGE Metal edging that fits on the edge of a roof to protect the fascia boards.

EASEMENT The legal right for one person (or entity) to cross or use another person's land. The most common easements are narrow tracts for utility lines.

ENGINEERED LUMBER Beams constructed from wood fiber and glue, such as Glu-lam, micro-lam, or wood I-beams. Often superior in strength and durability to dimension lumber.

FACENAIL To drive a nail through one piece into another with the nail at right angle to the surface.

FASCIA A trim piece fastened to the ends of the rafters to form part of the cornice.

FLASHING Material that seals a roof or wall at its vulnerable points, such as at the valley, eaves, and openings like vents.

FOOTING The lowest part of a concrete foundation, which distributes the weight of a structure.

FRIEZE BOARD Trim pieces installed directly beneath the rafters to provide a nailing surface for the soffits and corner trim.

FROST LINE The maximum depth to which the ground will freeze in a particular locale.

GIRDER A horizontal steel or wood member used to support part of a structure's load.

GIRT Horizontal perimeter timbers used in post-and-beam construction that function as nailers for vertical siding.

GUSSET PLATE Metal or plywood plate used to hold together the chords and webs of a truss.

HEADER A support piece that frames an opening in a floor, wall, ceiling, or roof at right angles to the other framing members; may be solid wood, built up from 2-by material, or engineered lumber.

JACK RAFTER A short rafter that runs between two rafters or a rafter and a top plate.

JACK STUD A stud that runs between the sole plate and the bottom of the header; also referred to as a trimmer stud.

JAMB The upright surface forming the side in an opening, as for a door or window.

JOIST Horizontal wooden framing member, usually 2-by lumber, placed on edge, as in a floor or ceiling joist.

KING STUD Stud to which the jack stud is attached to make a rough opening for a window or door.

KNEE BRACE Diagonal brace that's fastened between a beam and the top of a post for lateral stability.

LEDGER A structural member attached to a structure to support porch or deck joists.

LET-IN BRACING Diagonal brace (wood or metal) that keeps the walls square.

ON CENTER (OC) The spacing between framing members as measured from the center of one to the center of the next.

PIER A round or square concrete base used to support columns, posts, girders, or joists.

PLATE A horizontal framing member lying flat, usually made of 2-by lumber. Forms the top or bottom of a wall frame, as in the top or sole plate, respectively.

PLUMB Exactly vertical. Also, to make vertical.

POST-AND-BEAM FRAMING Identified by its use of large, widely spaced load-carrying timbers; also referred to as post-and-girt, post-and-lintel, or timber framing.

RAFTER An angled framing member that forms part of the sloping sides of a roof and supports the roof deck and roofing materials.

RAKE The inclined side of a gable.

RIM JOIST A type of joist fastened across the ends of other joists to keep the structure rigid.

RISE The vertical distance between the supporting wall's top plate and the point where a line, drawn through the outside edge

of the cap plate and parallel to the roof's edge, intersects the centerline of the ridge board.

ROUGH OPENING Opening in framing sized to accept a window or door prepared with a header and jack, king, and cripple studs to assume a structural load.

SETBACK A local building code requirement that structures be built a certain distance from the street, sidewalk, or property line.

SHEATHING The exterior skin of a structure under the siding or roofing, usually plywood.

SLOPE The rise of the roof over its run, expressed as the number of inches of rise per unit of run (typically 12 inches); 8 in 12 means a roof rises 8 inches for every 12 inches of run.

SOFFIT The area below the eaves, where the roof overhangs the exterior walls.

SPAN The distance that a member covers from the center of one supporting member to the center of the next.

TOENAIL To drive a nail at an angle through one piece and into another.

TRUSS An assembly of framing units that forms a rigid framework, typically for roofs.

shed and
garage plans

A NEW GARAGE OR SHED CAN solve your storage problems, provide a protected area for your car, and add charm to your property. If the projects featured earlier in this book weren't quite what you are looking for, or if you need more detailed building plans, then check out the plans for sale on the following pages. Whether you need a simple shed to house your garden tools or an elaborate garage that extends your living space, you'll find a wide variety of options. And if you build it yourself, you'll have the added satisfaction of watching the structure take shape with each saw cut and swing of the hammer. The opposite page provides all the ordering information you'll need. Just choose the plan that's right for you from the selection beginning on page 130 and call, fax or mail in your order; you'll be well on your way to an exciting new building project.

How To Order

For fastest service,
Call Toll-Free 1-800-367-7667
day or night

Three Easy Ways To Order

1. CALL toll free 1-800-367-7667 for credit card orders. MasterCard, Visa, Discover and American Express are accepted.

2. FAX your order to 1-314-770-2226.

3. MAIL the Order Form to:

   HDA, Inc.
   4390 Green Ash Drive
   St. Louis, MO 63045

QUESTIONS?
Call Our Customer Service Number
314-770-2228

ORDER FORM

Please send me -
PLAN NUMBER PB6-_____
           PRICE CODE _____ (see Plan Page)

Reproducible Masters (see chart at right) $_____
Initial Set of Plans $_____
Additional Plan Sets (see chart at right)
_____ (Qty) at $ _____ each $_____
                              Subtotal $_____
Sales Tax (MO residents add 7%) $_____
☐ Shipping / Handling (see chart at right) $_____
   (each additional set add $2.00 to shipping charges)

TOTAL ENCLOSED (US funds only) $_____

☐ Enclosed is my check or money order payable
   to HDA, Inc. (Sorry, no COD's)

I hereby authorize HDA, Inc. to charge this
purchase to my credit card account (check one):

☐ MasterCard ☐ VISA ☐ DISCOVER NOVUS ☐ AMERICAN EXPRESS Cards

Credit Card number _____

Expiration date _____

Signature _____

Name _____
           (Please print or type)

Street Address _____
                  (Please **do not** use PO Box)

City _____

State _____ Zip _____

Daytime phone number (_____) - _____

Thank you for your order!

IMPORTANT INFORMATION TO KNOW BEFORE YOU ORDER

• **Exchange Policies** - Since blueprints are printed in response to your order, we cannot honor requests for refunds. However, if for some reason you find that the plan you have purchased does not meet your requirements, you may exchange that plan for another plan in our collection. At the time of the exchange, you will be charged a processing fee of 25% of your original plan package price, plus the difference in price between the plan packages (if applicable) and the cost to ship the new plans to you.

Please note: Reproducible drawings can only be exchanged if the package is unopened, and exchanges are allowed only within 90 days of purchase.

• **Building Codes & Requirements** - At the time the construction drawings were prepared, every effort was made to ensure that these plans and specifications meet nationally recognized codes. Our plans conform to most national building codes. Because building codes vary from area to area, some drawing modifications and/or the assistance of a professional designer or architect may be necessary to comply with your local codes or to accommodate specific building site conditions. We advise you to consult with your local building official for information regarding codes governing your area.

BLUEPRINT PRICE SCHEDULE

Price Code	1-Set	Additional Sets	Reproducible Masters
P4	$20.00	$10.00	$70.00
P5	$25.00	$10.00	$75.00
P6	$30.00	$10.00	$80.00
P7	$50.00	$10.00	$100.00
P8	$75.00	$10.00	$125.00
P9	$125.00	$20.00	$200.00
P10	$150.00	$20.00	$225.00
P11	$175.00	$20.00	$250.00
P12	$200.00	$20.00	$275.00
P13	$225.00	$45.00	$440.00

Plan prices guaranteed through December 31, 2004.
Please note that plans are not refundable.

SHIPPING & HANDLING CHARGES
EACH ADDITIONAL SET ADD $2.00 TO SHIPPING CHARGES

U.S. SHIPPING

Regular (allow 7-10 business days)	$5.95
Priority (allow 3-5 business days)	$15.00
Express* (allow 1-2 business days)	$25.00

CANADA SHIPPING

Standard (allow 8-12 business days)	$15.00
Express* (allow 3-5 business days)	$40.00

OVERSEAS SHIPPING/INTERNATIONAL

Call, fax, or e-mail (plans@hdainc.com) for shipping costs.

* For express delivery please call us by 11:00 a.m. CST

Design #PB6-12008

GARDEN SHED

- Size - 12' wide x 10' deep
- Wood floor on gravel base
- Height floor to peak - 9'-9"
- Rear wall height - 7'-1 1/2"
- Features skylight windows for optimal plant growth
- Ample room for tool and lawn equipment storage
- Complete list of materials
- Step-by-step instructions

Price Code P5

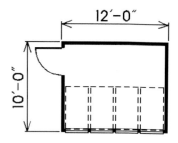

Design #PB6-12002

BARN STORAGE SHEDS WITH LOFT

- Three popular sizes -
  12' wide x 12' deep
  12' wide x 16' deep
  12' wide x 20' deep
- Wood floor on concrete pier foundation or concrete floor
- Height floor to peak - 12'-10"
- Ceiling height - 7'-4"
- 4'-0"x6'-8" double-door
- Complete list of materials
- Step-by-step instructions

Price Code P5

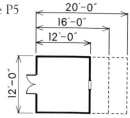

Design #PB6-12007

CONVENIENCE SHED

- Size - 16' wide x 12' deep
- Concrete floor
- Height floor to peak - 12'-4 1/2"
- Ceiling height - 8'-0"
- 8'-0"x7'-0" overhead door
- Ideal for lawn equipment or small boat storage
- Oversized windows brighten interior
- Complete list of materials
- Step-by-step instructions

Price Code P6

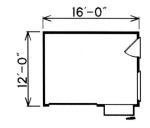

Design #PB6-12006

CHILDREN'S PLAYHOUSE

- Size - 8' wide x 8' deep
- Wood floor on 4x4 runners
- Height floor to peak - 9'-2"
- Ceiling height - 6'-1"
- 2' deep porch
- Attractive window boxes
- Includes operable windows
- Complete list of materials
- Step-by-step instructions

Price Code P4

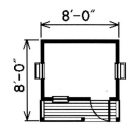

Design #PB6-12005

GABLE STORAGE SHEDS

- Three popular sizes -
  10' wide x 12' deep
  10' wide x 16' deep
  10' wide x 20' deep
- Wood floor on 4x4 runners
- Height floor to peak - 8'-8 1/2"
- Ceiling height - 7'-0"
- 4'-0"x6'-4" double-door for easy access
- Complete list of materials
- Step-by-step instructions

Price Code P5

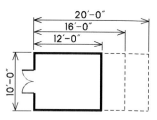

Design #PB6-12016

STORAGE SHED WITH PLAYHOUSE LOFT

- Size - 12' wide x 12' deep with 2'-8" deep balcony
- Wood floor on concrete piers or concrete floor
- Height floor to peak - 14'-1"
- Ceiling height - 7'-4"
- 4'-0"x6'-10" door
- Loft above can be used as playhouse for children
- Loft features ladder for easy access
- Complete list of materials
- Step-by-step instructions

Price Code P5

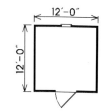

Design #PB6-12026

MINI BARNS

- Four popular sizes -
  8' wide x 8' deep
  8' wide x 10' deep
  8' wide x 12' deep
  8' wide x 16' deep
- Wood floor on 4x4 runners
- Height floor to peak - 7'-6"
- Ceiling height - 6'-0"
- 4'-0"x6'-0" double-door
- Storage of lawn and garden equipment
- Complete list of materials
- Step-by-step instructions

Price Code P5

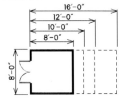

Design #PB6-12001

SALT BOX STORAGE SHEDS

- Three popular sizes -
  8' wide x 8' deep
  12' wide x 8' deep
  16' wide x 8' deep
- Wood floor on gravel base or concrete floor
- Height floor to peak - 8'-2"
- Front wall height - 7'-0"
- 6'-0"x6'-5" double-door for easy access
- Complete list of materials
- Step-by-step instructions

Price Code P5

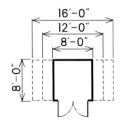

Design #PB6-12022

YARD BARN WITH LOFT STORAGE

- Size - 10' wide x 12' deep
- Wood floor on 4x4 runners
- Height floor to peak - 10'-7"
- Ceiling height - 6'-11"
- 6'-0"x6'-2" double-door for easy access
- Loft provides additional storage area
- Attractive styling suitable for yard
- Complete list of materials
- Step-by-step instructions

Price Code P5

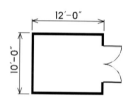

Design #PB6-12003

YARD BARNS

- Three popular sizes -
  10' wide x 12' deep
  10' wide x 16' deep
  10' wide x 20' deep
- Wood floor on 4x4 runners
- Height floor to peak - 8'-4 1/2"
- Ceiling height - 6'-4"
- 4'-0"x6'-4" double-door for easy access
- Ample storage area for lawn or garden equipment
- Complete list of materials
- Step-by-step instructions

Price Code P5

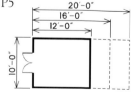

Design #PB6-12004

GABLE STORAGE SHEDS

- Four popular sizes -
  8' wide x 8' deep
  8' wide x 10' deep
  8' wide x 12' deep
  8' wide x 16' deep
- Wood floor on 4x4 runners
- Height floor to peak - 8'-4 1/2"
- Ceiling height - 7'-0"
- 4'-0" x 6'-5" double-door
- Economical and easy to build shed
- Complete list of materials
- Step-by-step instructions

Price Code P5

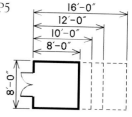

Design #PB6-12009

BARN STORAGE SHEDS

- Three popular sizes -
  12' wide x 8' deep
  12' wide x 12' deep
  12' wide x 16' deep
- Wood floor on concrete pier foundation or concrete floor
- Height floor to peak - 9'-10"
- Ceiling height - 7'-10"
- 5'-6"x6'-8" double-door
- Gambrel roof design
- Complete list of materials
- Step-by-step instructions

Price Code P5

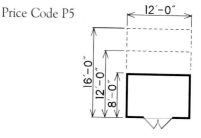

Design #PB6-12013

PLAYHOUSE/STORAGE SHED

- Size - 8' wide x 12' deep
- Wood floor on concrete piers or concrete floor
- Height floor to peak - 10'-6"
- Ceiling height - 7'-0"
- 3'-0"x6'-0" door
- Quaint chalet design
- Ideal playhouse in summer
- Storage shed in the off season
- Complete list of materials
- Step-by-step instructions

Price Code P4

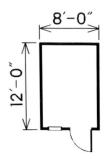

Design #PB6-12021

SALT BOX STORAGE SHED

- Size - 10' wide x 8' deep
- Wood floor on 4x4 runners
- Height floor to peak - 9'-6"
- Front wall height - 8'-0"
- 4'-0"x6'-8" double-door for easy access
- Window adds light to space
- Complete list of materials
- Step-by-step instructions

Price Code P5

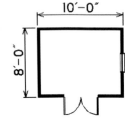

Design #PB6-12011

MINI BARN STORAGE SHEDS

- Four popular sizes -
  7'-3" wide x 6' deep   7'-3" wide x 8' deep
  7'-3" wide x 10' deep   7'-3" wide x 12' deep
- Wood floor on 4" x 6" runners or concrete floor
- Height floor to peak - 9'-0"
- Ceiling height - 7'-4"
- 3'-0"x6'-8" door
- Attractive styling with gambrel roof
- Complete list of materials
- Step-by-step instructions

Price Code P5

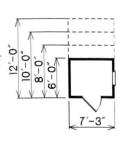

Design #PB6-12017

GARDEN SHEDS WITH CLERESTORY

- Three popular sizes -
  10' wide x 10' deep
  12' wide x 10' deep
  14' wide x 10' deep
- Wood floor on 4x6 runners
- Height floor to peak - 10'-11"
- Rear wall height - 7'-3"
- 5'-0"x6'-9" double-door
- Clerestory windows for added light
- Complete list of materials
- Step-by-step instructions

Price Code P5

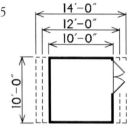

Design #PB6-12023

BARN STORAGE SHED WITH OVERHEAD DOOR

- Size - 12' wide x 16' deep
- Concrete floor
- Height floor to peak - 12'-5"
- Ceiling height - 8'-0"
- 8'-0"x7'-0" overhead door for easy entry with large equipment
- Side windows adds light to interior
- Complete list of materials
- Step-by-step instructions

Price Code P5

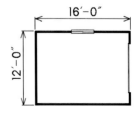

Design #PB6-12020

DELUXE CABANA

- Size - 11'-0" wide x 13'-6" deep
- Concrete floor
- Height floor to peak - 11'-7"
- Ceiling height - 8'-0"
- Unique roof design with skylight
- Convenient dressing room
- Perfect storage for poolside furniture and equipment
- Complete list of materials
- Step-by-step instructions

Price Code P6

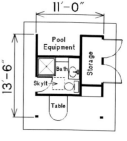

Design #PB6-12018

STORAGE SHED WITH LOG BIN

- Size - 10' wide x 6' deep
- Wood floor on gravel base
- Height floor to peak - 9'-7"
- Ceiling height - 6'-7"
- 5'-0"x6'-9" double-door for easy access
- Log storage area - 2'-6"x6'-0"
- Complete list of materials
- Step-by-step instructions

Price Code P5

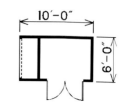

Design #PB6-12014

GREENHOUSE

- Size - 12' wide x 8' deep
- Gravel floor with concrete foundation wall
- Height foundation to peak - 8'-3"
- An attractive addition to any yard
- Store lawn and garden tools right at hand
- Complete list of materials
- Step-by-step instructions

Price Code P5

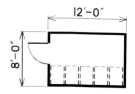

Design #PB6-12019

CHILDREN'S PLAYHOUSE

- Size - 6' wide x 6' deep
- Wood floor on gravel base
- Height floor to peak - 7'-2"
- Wall height - 4'-4"
- Plenty of windows brighten interior
- Attractive Victorian style
- Gabled doorway and window box add interest
- Complete list of materials
- Step-by-step instructions

Price Code P4

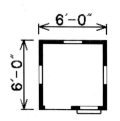

Design #PB6-12010

GABLE STORAGE SHEDS

- Three popular sizes -
  8' wide x 8' deep
  8' wide x 10' deep
  8' wide x 12' deep
- Wood floor on concrete footings
- Height floor to peak - 9'-1"
- Wall height - 6'-7"
- Circle-top window adds interest and light
- Complete list of materials
- Step-by-step instructions

Price Code P5

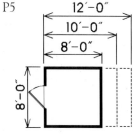

Design #PB6-12024

GABLE STORAGE
SHED/PLAYHOUSE

- Size - 12' wide x 8' deep
- Wood floor on 4x4 runners
- Height floor to peak - 10'-5"
- Ceiling height - 8'-0"
- 3'-0"x6'-8" dutch door
- Perfect for storage or playhouse for children
- Shutters and window box create a charming facade
- Complete list of materials
- Step-by-step instructions

Price Code P5

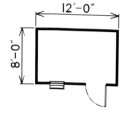

Design #PB6-12025

GARDEN SHED

- Size - 10' wide x 10' deep
- Wood floor on 4x4 runners
- Height floor to peak - 11'-3 1/2"
- Left wall height - 8'-0"
- Wonderful complement to any backyard
- Perfect space for lawn equipment or plants and flowers
- Plenty of windows for gardening year-round
- Complete list of materials
- Step-by-step instructions

Price Code P5

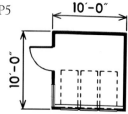

Design #PB6-14034

2 CAR ECONOMY GARAGE

- Size - 20' x 20'
- Building height - 11'-10"
- Roof pitch - 4/12
- Ceiling height - 8'-0"
- 16'x7' overhead door
- Convenient side-entry
- Complete list of materials
- Step-by-step instructions

Price Code P6

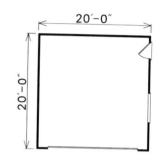

Design #PB6-14045

1 CAR GARAGE WITH LOFT, GAMBREL ROOF

- Size - 16' x 24'
- Building height - 18'-9"
- Roof pitch - 12/6, 6/12
- Ceiling height - 8'-0"
- Loft ceiling height - 6'-7"
- 9'x7' overhead door
- Handy side door and loft area
- Complete list of materials
- Step-by-step instructions

Price Code P8

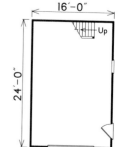

Design #PB6-14030

1 CAR GARAGES

- Four popular sizes -
  14' x 22'   14' x 24'
  16' x 22'   16' x 24'
- Building height - 11'-2"
- Roof pitch - 4/12
- Ceiling height - 8'-0"
- 9'x7' overhead door
- Sturdy, attractive design
- Complete list of materials
- Step-by-step instructions

Price Code P6

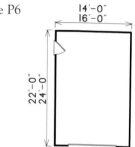

Design #PB6-14048

3 CAR GARAGE

- Size - 40' x 24'
- Building height - 15'-6"
- Roof pitch - 6/12
- Ceiling height - 9'-0"
- Three 9'x7' overhead doors
- Oversized with plenty of
  room for storage
- Side door for easy access
- Complete list of materials
- Step-by-step instructions

Price Code P7

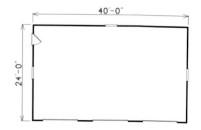

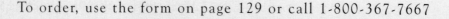

Design #PB6-14020

2 CAR GARAGE WITH
8' HIGH DOOR

- Size - 24' x 26'
- Building height - 13'-8"
- Roof pitch - 4/12
- Ceiling height - 9'-0"
- 16'x8' overhead door
- Practical and appealing
- Side window adds light
- Complete list of materials
- Step-by-step instructions

Price Code P7

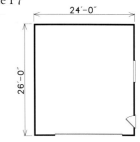

Design #PB6-14021

3 CAR GARAGE
WITH WORKSHOP

- Size - 32' x 28'
- Building height - 13'-3"
- Roof pitch - 4/12
- Ceiling height - 8'-0"
- 9'x7' and 16'x7' overhead doors
- Handy workshop space for hobbies
- Side-entry door provides easy access
- Complete list of materials
- Step-by-step instructions

Price Code P7

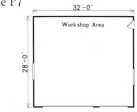

Design #PB6-14003

2 CAR GARAGE WITH WORKSHOP AND PARTIAL LOFT

- Size - 32' x 24'
- Building height - 20'-2"
- Roof pitch - 10/12
- Ceiling height - 9'-8"
- Workshop/loft ceiling height - 8'-0"
- 16'x7' overhead door, 6'-0"x6'-8" double-door
- Convenient loft above workshop for work space or storage
- Complete list of materials
- Step-by-step instructions

Price Code P8

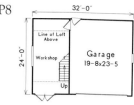

Design #PB6-14047

2 CAR CARPORT WITH STORAGE

- Size - 24' x 24'
- Building height - 12'-8"
- Roof pitch - 4/12
- Ceiling height - 8'-0"
- Unique design allows cars to enter from the front or the side of carport
- Deep storage space for long or tall items
- Complete list of materials
- Step-by-step instructions

Price Code P6

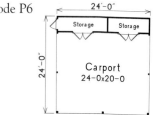

Design #PB6-14006

1 CAR GARAGE

- Size - 14' x 22'
- Building height - 10'-10"
- Roof pitch - 4/12
- Ceiling height - 8'-0"
- 9'x7' overhead door
- Side window enhances exterior
- Side-entry is convenient
- Complete list of materials
- Step-by-step instructions

Price Code P6

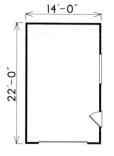

Design #PB6-14016

2 CAR GARAGE WITH LOFT

- Size - 26' x 24'
- Building height - 20'-0"
- Roof pitch - 6/12
- Ceiling height - 8'-0"
- Two 9'x7' overhead doors
- Loft provides extra storage area or workshop space
- Clerestory windows brighten inside
- Complete list of materials
- Step-by-step instructions

Price Code P8

Design #PB6-14014

2 CAR GARAGE

- Size - 22' x 22'
- Building height - 12'-2"
- Roof pitch - 4/12
- Ceiling height - 8'-0"
- 16'x7' overhead door
- Useful side-entry door
- Perfect for tractor or lawn equipment
- Complete list of materials
- Step-by-step instructions

Price Code P6

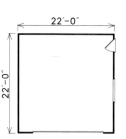

Design #PB6-14005

2 CAR GARAGE WITH WORKSHOP AND LOFT

- Size - 32' x 24'
- Building height - 21'-0"
- Roof pitch - 12/12
- Ceiling height - 8'-0"
- Loft ceiling height - 7'-6"
- Two 9'x7' overhead doors
- Plenty of storage space for workshop or hobby center
- Complete list of materials
- Step-by-step instructions

Price Code P8

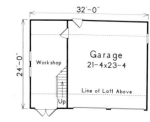

Design #PB6-15021

WORKROOM WITH COVERED PORCH

- Size - 24' x 20'
- Slab foundation
- Building height - 13'-6"
- Roof pitch - 6/12
- Ceiling height - 8'-0"
- Easy access through double-door entry
- Interior enhanced by large windows
- Large enough for storage
- Complete list of materials
- Step-by-step instructions

Price Code P8

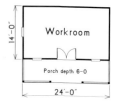

Design #PB6-14046

3 CAR GARAGE & LOFT

- Size - 36' x 24'
- Building height - 20'-8"
- Roof pitch - 12/12
- Ceiling height - 8'-0"
- Loft ceiling height - 7'-6"
- Three 9'x7' overhead doors
- Third stall in garage perfect for boat storage
- Generous loft space for storage or studio
- Complete list of materials
- Step-by-step instructions

Price Code P8

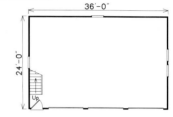

Design #PB6-14017

2 CAR GARAGE WITH STORAGE

- Size - 24' x 24'
- Building height - 12'-8"
- Roof pitch - 4/12
- Ceiling height - 8'-0"
- 16'x7' overhead door
- Windows and side-entry add appeal
- Functional and practical
- Complete list of materials
- Step-by-step instructions

Price Code P7

Design #PB6-14011

1 CAR GARAGE WITH COVERED PORCH

- Size - 24' x 22'
- Building height - 13'-0"
- Roof pitch - 5/12
- Ceiling height - 8'-0"
- 9'x7' overhead door
- Distinctive covered porch provides area for entertaining
- Complete list of materials
- Step-by-step instructions

Price Code P7

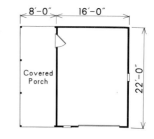

Design #PB6-14026

3 CAR GARAGE

- Size - 30' x 24'
- Building height - 13'-8"
- Roof pitch - 5/12
- Ceiling height - 8'-0"
- 16'-7", 9'x7' overhead doors
- Highly functional design
- Handy side-entry door
- Complete list of materials
- Step-by-step instructions

Price Code P7

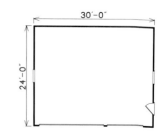

Design #PB6-14025

2 1/2 CAR GARAGE, WESTERN STYLE

- Size - 30' x 24'
- Building height - 12'-6"
- Roof pitch - 4/12
- Ceiling height - 8'-0"
- Two 9'x7' overhead doors
- Plenty of storage space
- Additional space perfect for workshop
- Complete list of materials
- Step-by-step instructions

Price Code P7

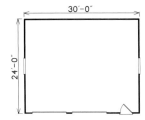

Design #PB6-15029

2 CAR GARAGE APARTMENT, GAMBREL ROOF

- 438 square feet
- Building height - 21'-3"
- Roof pitch - 6/12, 12/6
- Ceiling heights-
  1st Floor - 8'-0"   2nd Floor - 7'-9"
- Two 9'x7' overhead doors
- Comfortable colonial-styling
- Simple yet spacious studio design
- Complete list of materials
- Step-by-step instructions

Price Code P9

Design #PB6-15002

MULTI-PURPOSE BARN

- Size - 24' x 36'
- Building height - 23'-8"
- Roof pitch - 4/12, 12/4
- Two 9'x9' sliding doors
- 9'-9" loft ceiling height
- 5'x6' loft double-door
- Ideal machine storage or as a three-stall horse barn
- Loft designed for 100 p.s.f. live load
- Complete list of materials
- Step-by-step instructions

Price Code P8

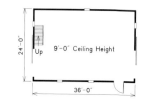

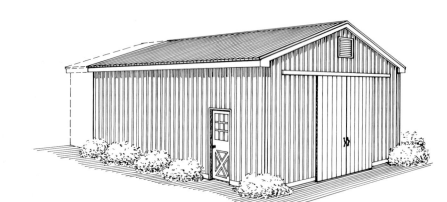

Design #PB6-15004

POLE BUILDINGS

- Four popular sizes -
  24' x 32'   24' x40'
  32' x 40'   32' x 48'
- Building height - 15'-6" with 10' ceiling height
- Building height - 17'-6" with 12' ceiling height
- Two 5'x10' or two 6'x12' sliding doors
- Designed for easy maintenance
- Complete list of materials
- Step-by-step instructions

Price Code P8

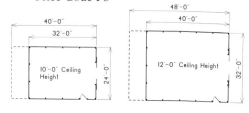

Design #PB6-14041

2 CAR GARAGE WITH LOFT AND FRONT DOOR

- Size - 28' x 24'
- Building height - 21'-0"
- Roof pitch - 12/12
- Ceiling height - 8'-0"
- Loft ceiling height - 7'-6"
- Two 9'x7' overhead doors
- Charming dormers add character
- Handy side door accessing stairs to loft
- Complete list of materials

Price Code P8

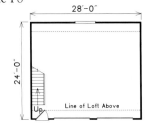

Design #PB6-14002

2 CAR GARAGE WITH LOFT

- Size - 28' x 24'
- Building height - 21'-0"
- Roof pitch - 12/12
- Ceiling height - 8'-0"
- Loft ceiling height - 7'-6"
- Two 9'x7' overhead doors
- Complete list of materials
- Step-by-step instructions

Price Code P8

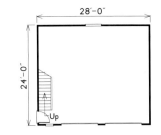

3 CAR GARAGE/WORKSHOP

- Size - 24' x 36'
- Building height - 14'-6"
- Roof pitch - 4/12
- Ceiling height - 10'-0"
- Three 9'x8' overhead doors
- Oversized for storage
- Ideal size for workshop or maintenance building
- Complete list of materials
- Step-by-step instructions

Price Code P7

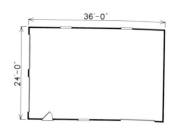

Design #PB6-14009

2 CAR GARAGE WITH STORAGE, REVERSE GABLE

- Size - 24' x 24'
- Building height - 12'-8"
- Roof pitch - 4/12
- Ceiling height - 8'-0"
- 16'x7' overhead door
- Windows on two sides
- Extra space perfect for storage
- Complete list of materials
- Step-by-step instructions

Price Code P7

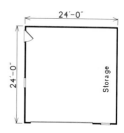

Design #PB6-14001

2 CAR GARAGE WITH LOFT, GAMBREL ROOF

- Size - 22' x 26'
- Building height - 20'-7"
- Roof pitch - 7/12, 12/7
- Ceiling height - 8'-0"
- Loft ceiling height - 7'-4"
- Two 9'x7' overhead doors
- Complete list of materials
- Step-by-step instructions

Price Code P8

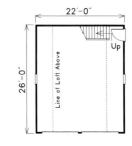

Design #PB6-14007

2 CAR GARAGE, REVERSE GABLE

- Size - 24' x 24'
- Building height - 16'-7"
- Roof pitch - 8/12
- Ceiling height - 8'-0"
- Two 9'x7' overhead doors
- Oversized, appealing design
- Side door is a handy feature
- Complete list of materials
- Step-by-step instructions

Price Code P7

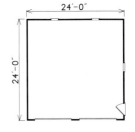

Design #PB6-14023

1 CAR GARAGE,
WESTERN STYLE

- Size - 14' x 22'
- Building height - 10'-10"
- Roof pitch - 4/12
- Ceiling height - 8'-0"
- 9'x7' overhead door
- Compact size, perfect for smaller lots
- Efficient side door provides easy access
- Complete list of materials
- Step-by-step instructions

Price Code P6

Design #PB6-14033

2 CAR GARAGE,
GAMBREL ROOF

- Size - 24' x 24'
- Building height - 15'-5"
- Roof pitch - 12/8, 4/12
- Ceiling height - 8'-0"
- 16'x7' overhead door
- Attractive addition to any home
- Complete list of materials
- Step-by-step instructions

Price Code P7

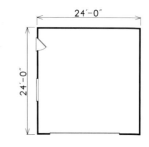

Design #PB6-14012

3 CAR GARAGE

- Size - 32' x 22'
- Building height - 12'-2"
- Roof pitch - 4/12
- Ceiling height - 8'-0"
- 9'x7' and 16'x7' overhead doors
- Side-entry for easy access
- Perfect style with many types of homes
- Complete list of materials
- Step-by-step instructions

Price Code P7

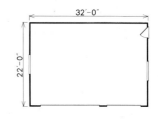

Design #PB6-14019

2 CAR GARAGE, VICTORIAN

- Size - 24' x 24'
- Building height - 16'-7"
- Roof pitch - 8/12
- Ceiling height - 8'-0"
- Two 9'x7' overhead doors
- Accented with Victorian details
- Functional side entry
- Complete list of materials
- Step-by-step instructions

Price Code P7

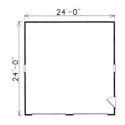

Design #PB6-15020

2 CAR GARAGE APARTMENT

- 784 square feet
- Building height - 24'-6"
- Roof pitch - 6/12
- Ceiling height - 8'-0"
- Two 9'x7' overhead doors
- 1 bedroom, 1 bath
- Open living area
- Space for utilities off the kitchen
- Complete list of materials
- Step-by-step instructions

Price Code P9

Design #PB6-15033

WORKSHOP WITH LOFT

- Size - 30' x 22'
- Slab foundation
- Building height - 20'-6"
- Roof pitch - 8/12, 6/12
- Ceiling height - 8'-0"
- 8'x7' overhead door
- Open floor plan has ample work space and additional storage with loft above
- Complete list of materials

Price Code P10

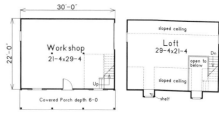

Design #PB6-15026

2 CAR GARAGE APARTMENT, GAMBREL ROOF

- 604 square feet
- Building height - 21'-4"
- Roof pitch - 4/12, 12/4.75
- Ceiling height - 8'-0"
- Two 9'x7' overhead doors
- Charming dutch colonial style
- Spacious studio provides extra storage space
- Complete list of materials
- Step-by-step instructions

Price Code P10

Design #PB6-15032

3 CAR GARAGE APARTMENT, CAPE COD

- 813 square feet
- Building height - 22'-0"
- Roof pitch - 12/12, 4.25/12
- Ceiling height - 8'-0"
- Three 9'x7' overhead doors
- Studio, 1 bath
- Spacious studio apartment with kitchen and bath
- Perfect for recreation, in-law or home office
- Complete list of materials

Price Code P12

Design #PB6-15011

2 CAR GARAGE APARTMENT WITH INTERIOR ENTRANCE

- 746 square feet
- Building height - 22'-0"
- Roof pitch - 4/12
- Ceiling height - 8'-0"
- Two 9'x7' overhead doors
- 1 bedroom, 1 bath
- Complete list of materials
- Step-by-step instructions

Price Code P9

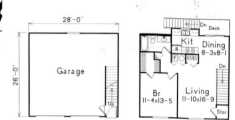

Design #PB6-15040

3-Car Apartment Garage, COUNTRY FLAIR

- 929 square feet
- Building height - 27'-0"
- Roof pitch - 6.5/12, 10/12
- Ceiling heights -
  1st floor - 9'-0"   2nd floor - 8'-0"
- 16' x 8', 9' x 8' overhead doors
- 2 bedrooms, 1 bath, 3-car side entry garage
- Slab foundation
- Complete list of materials

Price Code P13

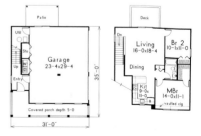

Design #PB6-15030

2 CAR GARAGE APARTMENT WITH EXTERIOR ENTRANCE

- 576 square feet
- Building height - 21'-5"
- Roof pitch - 4/12
- Ceiling height - 8'-0"
- Two 9'x7' overhead doors
- Roomy kitchen and dining area
- Private side exterior entrance
- Style complements many types of homes
- Complete list of materials
- Step-by-step instructions

Price Code P9

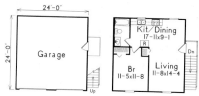

Design #PB6-15028

2 CAR GARAGE APARTMENT, CAPE COD

- 566 square feet
- Building height - 22'-0"
- Roof pitch - 12/12, 4.5/12
- Ceiling heights-
  1st floor - 8'-0"   2nd floor - 7'-7"
- Two 9'x7' overhead doors
- Charming dormers add appeal to this design
- Comfortable open living area
- Complete list of materials
- Step-by-step instructions

Price Code P10

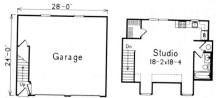

index